ALL FIRED UP

from the editors of **Southern Living**

with **Troy Black**, award-winning barbecue chef

ISBN-13: 978-0-8487-3648-4
ISBN-10: 0-8487-3648-6
Library of Congress Control Number: 2013930367

Printed in the United States of America
First Printing 2013

Oxmoor House
Editorial Director: Leah McLaughlin
Creative Director: Felicity Keane
Senior Brand Manager: Daniel Fagan
Senior Editor: Rebecca Brennan
Managing Editor: Rebecca Benton

Southern Living All Fired Up
Editor: Ashley T. Strickland
Art Director: Claire Cormany
Project Editor: Emily Chappell
Senior Designer: Melissa Clark
Director, Test Kitchen: Elizabeth Tyler Austin
Assistant Directors, Test Kitchen: Julie Christopher,
    Julie Gunter
Recipe Developers and Testers: Wendy Ball, R.D.;
    Victoria E. Cox; Tamara Goldis; Stefanie Maloney;
    Callie Nash; Karen Rankin; Leah Van Deren
Recipe Editor: Alyson Moreland Haynes
Food Stylists: Margaret Monroe Dickey,
    Catherine Crowell Steele
Photography Director: Jim Bathie
Senior Photographer: Hélène Dujardin
Senior Photo Stylist: Kay E. Clarke
Photo Stylist: Mindi Shapiro Levine
Assistant Photo Stylist: Mary Louise Menendez
Senior Production Manager: Susan Chodakiewicz
Assistant Production Manager: Diane Rose Keener

Time Home Entertainment Inc.
Publisher: Jim Childs
VP, Strategy & Business Development: Steven Sandonato
Executive Director, Marketing Services: Carol Pittard
Executive Director, Retail & Special Sales: Tom Mifsud
Director, Bookazine Development & Marketing:
    Laura Adam
Executive Publishing Director: Joy Butts
Associate Publishing Director: Megan Pearlman
Finance Director: Glenn Buonocore
Associate General Counsel: Helen Wan

Southern Living
Editor: M. Lindsay Bierman
Creative Director: Robert Perino
Managing Editor: Candace Higginbotham
Art Director: Chris Hoke
Executive Editors: Rachel Hardage Barrett,
    Hunter Lewis, Jessica S. Thuston
Food Director: Shannon Sliter Satterwhite
Senior Writer: Donna Florio
Senior Food Editor: Mary Allen Perry
Recipe Editor: JoAnn Weatherly
Assistant Recipe Editor: Ashley Arthur
Test Kitchen Specialist/Food Styling: Vanessa McNeil Rocchio
Test Kitchen Professionals: Norman King, Pam Lolley,
    Angela Sellers
Senior Photographers: Ralph Lee Anderson, Gary Clark,
    Art Meripol
Photographers: Robbie Caponetto, Laurey W. Glenn
Photo Research Coordinator: Ginny P. Allen
Senior Photo Stylist: Buffy Hargett
Editorial Assistant: Pat York

Contributors
Author: Troy Black
Recipe Developers and Testers: Erica Hopper, Tonya Johnson,
    Kyra Moncrief, Kathleen Royal Phillips
Copy Editors: Donna Baldone, Jacqueline Giovanelli
Proofreader: Adrienne Davis
Indexer: Mary Ann Laurens
Interns: Morgan Bolling, Susan Kemp, Alicia Lavender,
    Sara Lyon, Staley McIlwain, Emily Robinson, Maria Sanders,
    Katie Strasser
Food Stylist: Ana Kelly
Photographers: Cedric Angeles, Johnny Autry, Iain Bagwell,
    Sarah Belanger, Jennifer Davick, Peter Frank Edwards,
    Beau Gustafson, Beth Hontzas, Terry Manier,
    Meg McKinney, Chris M. Rogers, Mary Britton Senseney
Photo Stylists: Mary Clayton Carl, Caitlin Van Horn,
    Anna Pollock, Leslie Simpson

CONTENTS

WELCOME 7

TOOLS OF THE TRADE 9

SLATHERED AND SAUCED 20

AUTHENTIC BBQ 40

BEEF IT UP 84

PIG OUT 122

HOT CHIX 156

FRESH CATCH 190

SPECIAL EXTRAS 224

METRIC EQUIVALENTS 282

INDEX 283

All my life, I've had a love affair with food, fueled by the proud traditions of the wonderful Southern cooks in my family. Over the past several years, I've fulfilled my personal passion for barbecue and grilling by traveling the country, competing on the pro barbecue circuit. I've entered over 400 competitions, winning more than 100 first-place awards and numerous state championships in 11 different states.

Early in my journey in the barbecue and grilling world, I began to realize how much I enjoyed sharing my gifts as a professional barbecue pitmaster by teaching people how to create amazing barbecue at home. In this book, you'll find some of my favorite things to grill and barbecue, along with "how-to" steps so you can master the techniques. For me, barbecuing isn't just about the ingredients—it's about layering flavors with spices, marinades, sauces, and fire. It's more about knowing when it's done and not necessarily how long it takes to cook it.

There are many regional differences when it comes to barbecue. Visit Eastern North Carolina and you'll find the coastal side of the state has a drastically different sauce than the western side. If you like your barbecue sweet, Kansas City is the place to go. Or if you prefer barbecue chicken, Alabama has a delicious white sauce to complement it. People often ask me, "What part of the country is your favorite for barbecue?" They vary so much that my answer to that question is simply, "All of them!" To give you a taste from several regions, I've included recipes and tips from some of the best pitmasters around the country. You decide which is your favorite!

As you read this book, I hope you get a sense of my passion and love of creating delicious food. Whether you're making a mouthwatering steak grilled over a hot fire or a succulent pork shoulder, slow-smoked until it falls apart, you'll find yourself in a love affair similar to the one that started my journey.

Troy Black

TOOLS OF THE TRADE

THE SETUP

Before you start cooking, decide which grill and smoker work best for you.

GAS GRILLS

Gas grills are very easy to use and maintain consistent heat; they are especially handy for beginners. To turn them on, all you have to do is make sure that the propane valve is open, and with one slow turn of the knob, voilà, it's lit. To properly light a gas grill, turn all the burners to high, close the lid, and let the grill preheat for 10 to 15 minutes. Everyone has different needs to consider when buying a gas grill. If you like to grill out for the whole neighborhood or have a large household, you'll want to opt for a larger model with 4 to 5 burners. If you're just starting out and like to grill a couple times a week, I'd suggest a smaller version with 3 to 4 burners. Either way, every grill is different and some come with more bells and whistles than others.

CHARCOAL GRILLS

Charcoal grills can often be less expensive than gas grills. While they are typically more hands on, these grills have another advantage over gas grills in that they impart a characteristic smoky flavor. If you've got one of these grills, I highly recommend a chimney starter to help with lighting the coals. It will take about 15 to 30 minutes to get the coals lit, depending on the type of charcoal you use. Once the coals are lit, pour the coals into the bottom of the grill (below the grill grate), replace the grill grate, and cover the lid. Be sure that the air vents in the top and bottom are open. To increase the heat of the fire, open the vents wide. To decrease the heat, partially close the vents. Don't close the vents all the way unless you want the fire to go out.

SMOKERS

Water smokers (pictured) are probably the most common type of smoker since they are relatively inexpensive and fairly easy to operate. Most are bullet-shaped and come with a water pan. The water in the water pan acts as a temperature regulator and also often keeps meats that cook for a long period of time more moist. This type of smoker can consistently remain between the 200° and 250° range for up to 4 hours, and often longer, depending on what type of coals are used. This equipment creates an indirect cooking environment. The coals and wood are in the bottom section, the water pan in the middle, and the food in the top where the vents are also located.

Offset smokers are also readily available. This design has the charcoal and wood burning off to the side of the main cooking barrel with a vent for lowering or raising the heat. The location of the fuel chamber helps maintain an even cooking temperature for the main cooking barrel. There is also a "baffle" on top to help control the amount of air that comes in, which in turn helps regulate the amount of smoke.

TROY'S TIP

Resist the temptation to lift the lid during smoking to check meat before the recommended cooking time has elapsed; doing so allows heat and moisture to escape and adds to the cooking time.

TROY'S TOP 10 TOOLS

For barbecue success, make sure you have these must-have tools in your grilling tool kit.

1. Disposable Foil Pans Use these as a water pan, for soaking wood chips, and to even create your own homemade smoker box. You can also use them to take food to and from the grill.

2. Insulated Barbecue Mitts Be sure to invest in a pair of these. The insulated center will protect your hands from the high heat of the grill.

3. Chimney Starter If you plan to use a charcoal grill, you've got to have one of these. It makes lighting charcoal very simple, and you won't have to use lighter fluid (which often imparts a chemical flavor into your food). Look for one with a sturdy handle and large capacity.

4. Tongs This is my favorite tool to grab on to sturdier foods. I suggest having at least three pairs. One for placing raw foods on the grill, one for removing cooked foods, and one for adding more charcoal or wood chips to the fire. Spring-loaded tongs are often easiest to use, but any heavy-duty, dish washer-safe model will do.

5. Grill Brush To keep your grill grates clean, you'll need one of these. Look for a brush with stainless steel bristles, and use it to clean the grates before and after grilling so your food won't stick. If your grill happens to have cast-iron grates, you'll want to avoid this tool since it will clean off the seasoned coating.

6. Basting Brushes & Mops Have a bunch of these on hand for slathering on your favorite sauce, basting mixture, or marinade. There are many bristle options out there: synthetic or natural, cotton, and even silicone with beads at the tips. The silicone variety is dishwasher-safe.

7. Spatulas Collect several sizes and models of these to use to turn fish, burgers, and other grilled goodies with ease. Look for spatulas with long handles so your hands won't need to get so close to high heat.

8. Thermometers You'll want to have both an instant-read and an oven thermometer. The instant-read thermometer will ensure that you've cooked everything to proper doneness. While many grills offer built-in thermometers to showcase the heat of the interior, they are often inaccurate, as the location of these thermometers is not at the exact heat source. So, the actual temperature could really be much higher. For a more accurate reading, place the oven thermometer on the grill grate where the food will be cooked.

9. Kitchen Timer This tool is very handy, especially for those of us who are easily distracted and forget about our dinner on the grill outside. Look for models that are easy to read and count up as well as down for the most versatility.

10. Spray Bottle Fill with apple juice, vinegar, or other flavor-enhancers to spritz on meat as it cooks.

"the smoke is what makes the flavor"

Helen Turner

Helen's BBQ
Brownsville, TN

Helen Turner's gotten used to customers poking around her modest barbecue shack looking for the man who runs the place. But she's been stacking hickory and hoisting pork shoulders since 1995. Customers who aren't diverted by the idea of a female-run barbecue joint are often equally struck by the thick smoke that clouds the interior of Helen's BBQ. She tried installing fans to clear the air, but the pit's heat melted them. "Some people say sauce makes it special, but the smoke is what makes the flavor," Helen says. Helen cooks on an open pit; an effectively simple set up: bricks, metal fencing, hot coals, smoke and meat, all contained within a screened-in back porch.

Before Helen owned the place herself, she was a long-time employee of the restaurant. When the opportunity arose to make the business her own, Helen knew she couldn't turn it down. Although she is one of only a handful of female pitmasters in the country, she has put Helen's BBQ in the tiny town of Brownsville, Tennessee, on the map.

CHARCOAL

Basically, charcoal is pre-burned wood, and is available in two main varieties: charcoal briquettes and lump charcoal.

When folks began grilling, they did so over a wood fire, imparting a wonderful smoky flavor into foods. However, this type of fire creates an incredible amount of smoke and often requires a long wait time for the fire to die down enough to reach the desired temperature. So, charcoal was produced to prevent both of these drawbacks.

CHARCOAL BRIQUETTES

This type of charcoal is the most popular in the U.S. with a low price-point and ready availability. These little black nuggets are compressed sawdust, coal, and fillers like cornstarch. They create an even, easy-to-predict heat ideal for grilling over a long period of time. Also, because of their long burn time and steady heat, they produce a great smoking set up. But beware: Some briquettes are sold presoaked in lighter fluid to help start more easily. I wouldn't recommend using this variety. If you're not careful to burn off the lighter fluid completely, it will impart a chemical taste to your food.

Charcoal Briquettes

Lump Charcoal

LUMP CHARCOAL

When wood logs are slowly burned in a pit or kiln, the water and resins are removed to create charcoal, also known as big pieces of combustible carbon. These lumps are easy to light and create a relatively even range of heat. They also emit a flavorful smoke reflective of the type of wood from which they are made. Be sure you know what you're buying though. The bag should tell you what type of wood it is. Be sure to select those that are filled with big lumps of charcoal, about the size of an apple.

HOW TO PREPARE A CHARCOAL GRILL

1. Fill the bottom of a chimney starter with a few pieces of crumpled newspaper. Pour charcoal over the newspaper (fill entirely for a longer-burning fire). Light the newspaper through the holes in the chimney.

2. Let the charcoal burn until it is lightly coated with ash. For lump charcoal, it will take about 15 minutes; for briquettes, it will take about 20 to 30 minutes.

3. Remove the grill grates and pour the lit coals into the bottom of the grill. For direct grilling, spread the coals in an even layer. For indirect grilling, pile them to one side.

4. To prepare coals without a chimney starter, build a pyramid of coals and light them, starting in the middle. Once lit, pile others on top. The fire is ready when all the coals are bright orange and coated with ash. Arrange coals according to step 3.

TROY'S TIP

When following quick-grilling recipes, if space allows, I like to keep one side of the grill for indirect grilling. That way, if you have a flare-up, you can easily move the food to the cooler side and avoid overcooking or burning.

DIRECT OR INDIRECT

So you've got your grill ready to go, now what? Well, you'll want to determine if the recipe you're making calls for a direct or an indirect cooking method. Both can be done on either a gas or charcoal grill.

DIRECT HEAT

With direct grilling, food is cooked hot and fast directly over the fire. This method works best with thin and tender cuts of meat like burgers, steaks, vegetables, and fish. Don't try to cook a large roast using this method—the outside of the meat will likely burn before the inside is cooked.

For direct grilling using a gas grill, simply turn the knob of the burner to the desired temperature and cook the food directly over the heat source. If using a charcoal grill, spread the lit coals in one even layer on the bottom of the grill.

INDIRECT HEAT

With indirect heat, food is cooked low and slow beside the fire. Often, the meat is seared first directly over the fire, and then moved to the side to finish cooking, or it can be cooked all on the indirect side. This method is ideal for whole chickens, large roasts, and pork shoulder. It's what I call "authentic barbecue."

For indirect heat using a gas grill, light the burners on one side of the grill and place the meat on the unlit side. If using a charcoal grill, pile the lit coals to one side of the grill, replace the grill grate, and place the food over the unlit side.

"You want the wood to speak to you"

Will Fleischman

**Lockhart Smokehouse
Dallas, TX**

Will Fleischman has studied literature and worked as a chef in China. He has trained under a cattle rancher who sold beef to Leavenworth prison and a 350-pound man known as Pappy. But nothing daunts him like a brisket nearing the end of its run in a smoker. "The question of 'How do you know when it's done?' is where insecurity lives," he says. "You want the wood to speak to you, but the meat sits there in mute defiance."

Will doesn't rely on "cowboy wisdom" which equates pounds and cook time. Instead, he relies on instincts he's honed over the years. It's these instincts that have led him to become one of the South's best pitmasters. "People need to humble themselves to the experience," he says. "Success depends on how many mistakes you're willing to make."

Will currently works as the pitmaster and chef at Lockhart Smokehouse in Dallas, Texas, where he carries on the tradition of bringing the amazing smells and flavors that the people of Dallas have loved for years.

PITMASTER

WOOD

Another thing that makes authentic Southern barbecue great is the massive amount of flavor you can impart from the type of wood you use in smoking recipes. From peach and apple to mesquite and hickory, there are many different options available.

WOOD CHIPS

For smokers with small baskets, wood chips or small wood chunks are ideal. Be sure to soak them in water for at least 30 minutes, or else they'll catch on fire. They burn for about 20 minutes, and it's easy to add more to a charcoal fire or to a smoker box if they run out before you'd like. Add a handful or two for an additional 10 to 20 minutes of smoke time.

WOOD CHUNKS

For smokers with large fire baskets or chambers, you'll want to use larger wood chunks. These can range in size from as small as golf balls to as big as grapefruits. Wood chunks will burn for about 2 hours when placed over charcoal (they're too large to place in most smoker boxes).

SMOKING BASICS

It is a lot easier to smoke foods than you might think. If you're using a water smoker, the water acts as a temperature regulator and also keeps the environment moist, which in turn equals a juicier finished product. Simply pour water into the water pan to the fill line and place it in the smoker. Place soaked chips directly over hot coals and close the lid tightly to smoke.

If you're using a gas or charcoal grill to smoke, you can still achieve a delicious result. For gas grills, you'll want to use a smoker box. Place soaked wood chips into the smoker box and close the lid tightly. If you don't have a smoker box, you can make your own by placing soaked chips in a disposable foil pan and covering tightly with heavy-duty aluminum foil. Poke several holes in the foil to allow the smoke to escape. For smoking in a charcoal grill, place soaked chips or chunks directly onto the hot coals and cover the grill lid tightly. Add more charcoal, chips, or chunks as needed.

SLATHERED AND SAUCED

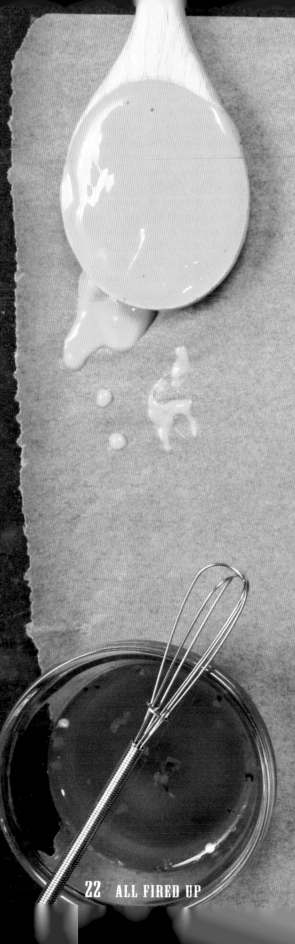

CAROLINA MUSTARD BBQ SAUCE

Makes: 1½ cups Hands-On Time: 6 min. Total Time: 51 min.

Mop this sweet-and-tangy sauce on chicken during the last 10 to 15 minutes of grilling.

1	cup yellow mustard	¼	cup cider vinegar
¼	cup firmly packed light brown sugar	½	tsp. kosher salt
¼	cup honey	½	tsp. coarsely ground pepper

1. Whisk together all ingredients in a medium saucepan. Bring to a boil; reduce heat, and simmer 15 minutes, whisking occasionally. Let cool 30 minutes or to room temperature.

EASTERN CAROLINA VINEGAR SAUCE

Makes: 3 cups Hands-On Time: 16 min. Total Time: 46 min.

Use this sauce for basting, or serve with pulled pork.

2	cups cider vinegar	1	Tbsp. kosher salt
½	cup white vinegar	1½	tsp. freshly ground black pepper
½	cup apple juice	½	tsp. paprika
¼	cup firmly packed brown sugar	½	tsp. dried crushed red pepper

1. Whisk together all ingredients in a medium saucepan. Bring to a boil over high heat, stirring until sugar melts. Let cool 30 minutes or to room temperature.

KANSAS CITY BBQ SAUCE

Makes: 2½ cups
Hands-On Time: 1 hour, 12 min.   **Total Time:** 1 hour, 42 min.

In Kansas City, folks like their barbecue sweet, and this sauce delivers. It's sweet and slightly tangy—perfect for ribs, pulled pork, and chops.

1	(6-oz.) can tomato paste	1	tsp.	Worcestershire sauce
½	cup cider vinegar	½	tsp.	kosher salt
¾	cup light corn syrup	½	tsp.	garlic powder
3	Tbsp. dark molasses	½	tsp.	freshly ground pepper
3	Tbsp. brown sugar	¼	tsp.	paprika

1. Whisk together all ingredients and 2 cups water in a medium saucepan. Bring to a boil over medium heat; reduce heat, and simmer, uncovered, 1 hour or until thickened, stirring occasionally. Let cool 30 minutes or to room temperature.

WHITE BBQ SAUCE

Makes: about 1¾ cups   **Hands-On Time:** 5 min.   **Total Time:** 5 min.

Made famous in Alabama, this sauce is perfect served with smoked chicken.

1½	cups mayonnaise	½	tsp.	salt
⅓	cup white vinegar	½	tsp.	sugar
1	tsp. freshly ground pepper	1		garlic clove, pressed

1. Stir together all ingredients in a small bowl. Store in the refrigerator.

ASIAN SEAFOOD MARINADE

Makes: about ¾ cup   Hands-On Time: 15 min.   Total Time: 15 min.

This recipe makes enough marinade for about 2 pounds of fish or seafood. Fish needs to marinate only about 1 hour, but peeled shrimp can go up to 2 hours.

⅓ cup dark sesame oil
¼ cup fresh lime juice
1 Tbsp. brown sugar
3 Tbsp. mirin
3 Tbsp. soy sauce

1 tsp. minced garlic
½ tsp. toasted sesame seeds
½ tsp. freshly ground black pepper
¼ tsp. dried crushed red pepper

1. Whisk together all ingredients until blended.

SWEET-AND-SPICY MARINADE

Makes: 2⅔ cups   Hands-On Time: 8 min.   Total Time: 8 min.

The flavors mellow as this mixture stands, so make it a few hours before you plan to grill. It's tasty on pork and chicken.

1 cup ketchup
⅔ cup firmly packed brown sugar
½ cup orange juice
⅓ cup Dijon mustard

1 Tbsp. Worcestershire sauce
1 Tbsp. balsamic vinegar
2 tsp. dried crushed red pepper

1. Whisk together all ingredients in a medium saucepan. Bring to a boil, and cook, whisking occasionally, 5 minutes. Cool completely before using as a marinade.

BEEF MARINADE

Makes: ⅔ cup   Hands-On Time: 5 min.   Total Time: 5 min.

¼ cup balsamic vinegar
2 Tbsp. soy sauce
2 Tbsp. honey

2 green onions, thinly sliced
2 tsp. chopped fresh rosemary
1½ tsp. Dijon mustard

1. Whisk together all ingredients until blended.

Asian Seafood Marinade

Sweet-and-Spicy
Marinade

Beef Marinade

LEMON-DIJON MARINADE

Makes: about 2½ cups   Hands-On Time: 10 min.   Total Time: 10 min.

1 cup vegetable oil	2 Tbsp. hot sauce
1 cup red wine vinegar	2 Tbsp. Dijon mustard
2 Tbsp. grated lemon rind	2 garlic cloves, pressed
¼ cup fresh lemon juice	½ tsp. salt
3 Tbsp. sugar	

1. Whisk together all ingredients.

NOTE: To prepare ahead, store in an airtight container in the refrigerator up to 1 week. Bring to room temperature, and whisk before using.

SRIRACHA RÉMOULADE

Makes: 2 cups   Hands-On Time: 10 min.   Total Time: 1 hour, 10 min.

1½ cups mayonnaise	2 to 3 Tbsp. Asian Sriracha hot chili sauce
4 green onions, sliced	1 garlic clove, pressed
2 Tbsp. chopped fresh parsley	

1. Whisk together all ingredients. Chill 1 hour, and store in an airtight container in the refrigerator up to 3 days.

MANGO KETCHUP

Makes: ¾ cup   Hands-On Time: 5 min.   Total Time: 5 min.

½ cup ketchup	¼ cup mango chutney

1. Whisk together all ingredients.

PORK DRY RUB

Makes: about 3½ cups
Hands-On Time: 5 min.   Total Time: 5 min.

This classic dry rub is also delicious on chicken, fish, and vegetables. It will keep more than a year when stored in an airtight container in a cool, dry place.

1	cup firmly packed dark brown sugar	2	Tbsp. ground chipotle chile pepper
1	cup paprika	1	Tbsp. chili powder
½	cup granulated garlic	1	Tbsp. ground cumin
½	cup kosher salt	1	Tbsp. freshly ground black pepper
2	Tbsp. dried minced onion		
2	Tbsp. ground red pepper	1	Tbsp. dry mustard

1. Stir together all ingredients in a medium bowl.

MEMPHIS DRY RUB

Makes: about ¾ cup   Hands-On Time: 8 min.   Total Time: 8 min.

Memphis barbecue is synonymous with ribs and pulled pork seasoned with highly flavorful rubs, smoked, and then served with sauce on the side.

⅓	cup paprika	1	tsp. freshly ground black pepper
2	Tbsp. granulated sugar		
2	Tbsp. dark brown sugar	1	tsp. dry mustard
2	tsp. salt	1	tsp. onion powder
2	tsp. garlic powder	1	tsp. ground red pepper
1	tsp. kosher salt		

1. Stir together all ingredients in a small bowl. Store in an airtight container in a cool, dark place up to 6 months.

ALL-PURPOSE BBQ RUB

Makes: 1 cup   Hands-On Time: 5 min.   Total Time: 5 min.

- ¼ cup firmly packed light brown sugar
- 2 Tbsp. granulated garlic
- 2 Tbsp. kosher salt
- 2 Tbsp. coarsely ground pepper
- 2 Tbsp. paprika
- 2 tsp. onion powder
- 1 tsp. ground cumin
- 1 tsp. dried basil
- 1 tsp. dried oregano
- 1 tsp. dried thyme

1. Stir together all ingredients in a small bowl. Store in an airtight container in a cool, dark place up to 6 months.

SMOKY-SWEET BBQ RUB

Makes: 1 cup   Hands-On Time: 5 min.   Total Time: 5 min.

- ¼ cup kosher salt
- ¼ cup firmly packed dark brown sugar
- 2 Tbsp. plus 2 tsp. smoked paprika
- 2 Tbsp. granulated sugar
- 2 tsp. garlic powder
- 2 tsp. freshly ground pepper
- 1 tsp. dry mustard
- 1 tsp. ground cumin
- 1 tsp. ground ginger

1. Stir together all ingredients. Store in an airtight container up to 1 month.

BRISKET DRY RUB

Makes: 2 cups   Hands-On Time: 10 min.   Total Time: 10 min.

- ¾ cup paprika
- ¼ cup kosher salt
- ¼ cup sugar
- ¼ cup freshly ground black pepper
- 2 Tbsp. chili powder
- 2 Tbsp. onion powder
- 2 Tbsp. ground chipotle chile pepper
- 2 Tbsp. ancho chile powder
- 1½ Tbsp. garlic powder
- 2 tsp. ground red pepper

1. Stir together all ingredients in a medium bowl. Store in an airtight container in a cool, dark place up to 6 months.

GRILLED SALSA

Makes: 4 cups **Hands-On Time: 30 min.** **Total Time: 45 min.**

2   ears fresh corn, husks removed
½   jalapeño pepper, seeded (optional)
1   small sweet onion, cut into ¼-inch-thick slices
6   medium tomatoes, halved (about 2 lb.)
Vegetable cooking spray

1   small garlic clove, quartered
¼   cup loosely packed fresh cilantro leaves
2   Tbsp. fresh lime juice
1½ tsp. salt
Fried pork rinds

1. Preheat grill to 350° to 400° (medium-high) heat. Coat corn, jalapeño pepper, if desired, onion, and cut sides of tomatoes lightly with cooking spray. Grill corn and onion, covered with grill lid, 15 minutes or until golden brown, turning occasionally. At the same time, grill tomatoes and jalapeño pepper, covered with grill lid, 8 minutes or until grill marks appear, turning occasionally. Remove all from grill, and cool 15 minutes. Cut corn kernels from cobs; discard cobs. Coarsely chop onion.

2. Pulse garlic and next 2 ingredients in a food processor until finely chopped. Add grilled tomatoes, onion, and jalapeño pepper to food processor, in batches, and pulse each batch until well blended. Transfer to a large bowl. Stir in salt and corn. Serve with pork rinds.

CHIPOTLE-MANGO SALSA

Makes: 2 cups   **Hands-On Time: 25 min.**   **Total Time: 25 min.**

Serve as a topping for chicken, pork, or fish, or as a dip with tortilla chips.

1¼ cups peeled and chopped mango
⅓ cup chopped red onion
⅓ cup chopped red bell pepper
⅓ cup fresh lime juice
2 Tbsp. honey
¼ cup chopped fresh cilantro

1 Tbsp. minced canned chipotle pepper in adobo sauce
1 tsp. kosher salt
¼ tsp. coarsely ground black pepper
2 garlic cloves, minced

1. Stir together all ingredients in a medium bowl. Cover and chill until ready to serve.

≈ HOW TO CHOP A MANGO ≈

CANTALOUPE-BACON RELISH

Makes: about 2½ cups   Hands-On Time: 20 min.   Total Time: 20 min.

Serve this relish over salad greens topped with sliced grilled chicken, or try it on grilled crostini with goat cheese as an appetizer.

1½ cups finely diced cantaloupe
½ cup seeded, diced cucumber
5 bacon slices, cooked and crumbled
1 green onion, minced
1 Tbsp. chopped fresh mint

2 Tbsp. extra virgin olive oil
2 to 3 tsp. red wine vinegar
¼ tsp. freshly ground pepper
Pinch of salt

1. Combine all ingredients. Serve immediately.

VIDALIA ONION AND PEACH REFRIGERATOR RELISH

Makes: about 10 (8-oz.) jars   Hands-On Time: 1 hour, 10 min.   Total Time: 3 hours, 25 min.

Take advantage of seasonal fruit and vegetables by sealing in their flavors at their peak. Preserve jars of refrigerator relish for family and friends to enjoy year-round.

2 cups sugar
2 cups cider vinegar
¼ cup gin
2 Tbsp. salt
1 Tbsp. mustard seeds
1 tsp. celery salt

½ tsp. dried crushed red pepper
4 bay leaves, crushed
3 lb. Vidalia onions, finely chopped
3 lb. fresh peaches, peeled and chopped
4 garlic cloves, thinly sliced

1. Bring 2 cups water, sugar, vinegar, gin, salt, mustard seeds, celery salt, dried crushed red pepper, and crushed bay leaves to a boil in a Dutch oven over medium-high heat. Add Vidalia onions, peaches, and garlic; boil, stirring occasionally, 15 minutes. Let mixture cool completely (about 2 hours). Store in airtight containers in refrigerator up to 2 weeks.

"Uniting the nation through barbecue"

Heath Hall

Pork Barrel BBQ
Washington, D.C.

In June of 2008, former United States Senate staffers Heath Hall and Brett Thompson turned their dreams into reality by filling the good barbecue void in the nation's capital. The pair launched their soon-to-be-famous Pork Barrel's All-American Spice Rub and joined forces with others as The Pork Barrel BBQ Competition BBQ Team to compete in the national barbecue circuit.

Heath and Brett have traveled all over the country competing in barbecue cook-offs and championships such as Memphis in May, The American Royal Invitational, and the Jack Daniels World Championships. They have won dozens of awards across many categories—Chicken, Ribs, Pork, and Brisket, and continue to gain applause and recognition for their barbecue sauces. In fact, their sauce was named "Best BBQ Sauce in the Nation" by *Men's Health* magazine.

Between appearances on ABC's *Shark Tank*, and other network news broadcasts, Heath and Brett strive to "unite the nation through the great tradition of barbecue, and bring bipartisan flavor to your next meal."

CHARRED GUACAMOLE WITH GRILLED CORN

Makes: 3¼ cups   Hands-On Time: 23 min.   Total Time: 50 min.

Although this tasty mixture is the perfect sidekick for tortilla chips, it's equally delicious piled on top of south-of-the-border-seasoned grilled chicken or steak.

- 2 ears fresh corn, husks removed
- 1 small red onion, cut into ½-inch-thick slices
- 3 avocados, halved
- 2 Tbsp. olive oil
- 1¼ tsp. Pork Barrel BBQ All-American Spice Rub or your favorite spice rub, divided
- ¼ cup chopped fresh cilantro
- ¼ cup fresh lime juice
- 2 garlic cloves, minced

1. Preheat grill to 350° to 400° (medium-high) heat. Brush corn, onion slices, and cut sides of avocados with oil; sprinkle with 1 tsp. rub. Grill corn, covered with grill lid, 12 minutes or until done, turning occasionally. At the same time, grill onion, covered with grill lid, 4 minutes on each side. Grill avocado, cut sides down, covered with grill lid, 3 minutes. Remove from grill; cool 15 minutes.

2. Stir together remaining ¼ tsp. rub, cilantro, lime juice, and garlic in a medium bowl. Hold each ear of corn upright on a cutting board; carefully cut downward, cutting kernels from cob. Add kernels to cilantro mixture in bowl; discard cobs. Chop onion and avocado; add to bowl. Mash mixture with a fork or potato masher just until chunky. Serve immediately.

RECIPE provided by Heath Hall of Pork Barrel BBQ.

MUFFULETTA DIP

Makes: about 4 cups   Hands-On Time: 10 min.   Total Time: 1 hour, 10 min.

Serve this dip with toasted French bread slices or as a topping for grilled chicken or fish.

1   cup Italian olive salad, drained
1   cup diced salami (about 4 oz.)
¼   cup grated Parmesan cheese
¼   cup chopped pepperoncini salad peppers
1   (2¼-oz.) can sliced black olives, drained

4   oz. provolone cheese, diced
1   celery rib, finely chopped
½   red bell pepper, chopped
1   Tbsp. olive oil
¼   cup chopped fresh parsley

1. Stir together first 9 ingredients. Cover and chill 1 to 24 hours before serving. Stir in parsley just before serving. Store leftovers in refrigerator up to 5 days.

NOTE: We tested with Boscoli Italian Olive Salad.

TROY'S TIP

Italian olive salad is a combination of olives and assorted pickled vegetables, like cauliflower and carrots. The vibrant colors of the vegetables and tanginess of the dip provide a tasty enhancement to a variety of grilled meats.

AUTHENTIC BBQ

TEXAS SMOKED BRISKET

Makes: 12 to 14 servings   Hands-On Time: 20 min.   Total Time: 6 hours, 40 min.

½   cup Brisket Dry Rub (page 29)
1   (6½-lb.) flat-cut brisket

Brisket Red Sauce

1. Soak wood chips in water 30 minutes. Prepare smoker according to manufacturer's directions, bringing internal temperature to 225° to 250°; maintain temperature for 15 to 20 minutes. Sprinkle Brisket Dry Rub on brisket, patting to adhere the rub. Let the brisket stand 10 minutes. Drain the wood chips, and place them on the coals. Place brisket on upper food rack; cover with smoker lid.

2. Smoke brisket, maintaining temperature inside smoker between 225° and 250°, for 5½ to 6 hours or until a meat thermometer inserted into thickest portion of brisket registers between 195° and 205°. Add additional charcoal and wood chips as needed. Remove brisket from smoker, and let stand 10 minutes. Cut brisket across the grain into thin slices, and serve with Brisket Red Sauce.

BRISKET RED SAUCE

Makes: 3¼ cups   Hands-On Time: 10 min.   Total Time: 10 min.

1½ cups cider vinegar
1   cup ketchup
½   cup firmly packed light brown sugar
¼   cup Worcestershire sauce
2   Tbsp. unsalted butter
1   tsp. salt

1½ tsp. onion powder
1½ tsp. granulated garlic
1½ tsp. ground cumin
½   tsp. freshly ground black pepper
½   tsp. ground red pepper

1. Whisk together all ingredients in a medium saucepan. Bring to a boil over high heat, stirring until butter melts. Remove from heat; serve warm.

COWBOY NACHOS

Makes: 6 to 8 servings   **Hands-On Time: 51 min.**   **Total Time: 51 min.**

Load these nachos with braised brisket and Monterey Jack cheese. Add all of your favorite classic nacho toppings to complete this savory appetizer.

2   (16-oz.) cans seasoned pinto beans, drained
2   tsp. hot sauce
1   tsp. minced garlic
½   tsp. freshly ground pepper
3½ cups shredded Texas Smoked Brisket
       (without sauce) (page 42)
1   Tbsp. canola oil

½   cup taco sauce
¼   cup beef broth
1   (9-oz.) package round tortilla chips
1   (8-oz.) block Monterey Jack cheese, shredded
Pico de Gallo
Toppings: guacamole, sour cream, pickled jalapeño
       pepper slices

1. Preheat oven to 425°. Cook first 4 ingredients and ½ cup water in a medium saucepan, stirring occasionally, over medium-low heat 5 to 7 minutes or until thoroughly heated.

2. Cook brisket in hot oil in a skillet over medium heat, stirring often, 4 minutes or until thoroughly heated. Stir in taco sauce and broth; cook 2 minutes.

3. Divide chips, bean mixture, brisket mixture, cheese, and 1 cup Pico de Gallo among 3 pie plates.

4. Bake at 425° for 5 minutes or until cheese is melted. Serve immediately with remaining Pico de Gallo and desired toppings.

PICO DE GALLO

Makes: 3½ cups   **Hands-On Time: 15 min.**   **Total Time: 15 min.**

6   plum tomatoes, chopped
½   cup finely chopped sweet onion
¼   cup chopped fresh cilantro
1   jalapeño pepper, seeded and minced

2   Tbsp. fresh lime juice
1   garlic clove, minced
½   tsp. salt

1. Combine all ingredients in a medium bowl. Cover and chill until ready to serve.

NOTE: Nachos can be baked as directed in 2 batches on an aluminum foil-lined baking sheet, topping each batch with 1 cup Pico de Gallo.

CHICKEN-AND-BRISKET BRUNSWICK STEW

Makes: 16 cups   Hands-On Time: 30 min.   Total Time: 2 hours, 40 min.

- 2   large onions, chopped
- 2   garlic cloves, minced
- 1   Tbsp. vegetable oil
- 1½ Tbsp. jarred beef soup base
- 2   lb. skinned and boned chicken breasts
- 1   (28-oz.) can fire-roasted crushed tomatoes
- 1   (12-oz.) package frozen white shoepeg or whole kernel corn
- 1   (10-oz.) package frozen cream-style corn, thawed

- 1   (9-oz.) package frozen baby lima beans
- 1   (12-oz.) bottle chili sauce
- 1   Tbsp. brown sugar
- 1   Tbsp. yellow mustard
- 1   Tbsp. Worcestershire sauce
- ½   tsp. coarsely ground pepper
- 1   lb. chopped Texas Smoked Brisket (without sauce) (page 42)
- 1   Tbsp. fresh lemon juice
- Hot sauce (optional)

1. Sauté onion and garlic in hot oil in a 7.5-qt. Dutch oven over medium-high heat 3 to 5 minutes or until tender. Combine soup base and 2 cups water; add to Dutch oven. Add chicken and next 9 ingredients. Bring to a boil. Cover, reduce heat to low, and cook, stirring occasionally, 2 hours.

2. Uncover and shred chicken into large pieces using 2 forks. Stir in brisket and lemon juice. Cover and cook 10 minutes. Serve with hot sauce, if desired.

TROY'S TIP

Be sure to shred the chicken while it's still hot. Using forks will prevent you from burning your fingers, and the chicken will easily separate into tender pieces.

BRISKET SHOOTERS

Makes: 12 servings   Hands-On Time: 40 min.   Total Time: 40 min.

If you don't have any leftover Texas Smoked Brisket, pick up some from your favorite local barbecue joint.

2	cups milk	1½ lb. shredded Texas Smoked Brisket (without sauce) (page 42)
1	cup uncooked regular grits	Coleslaw
½	tsp. salt	Barbecue sauce
1	cup (4 oz.) shredded smoked Gouda cheese	Garnish: fresh cilantro leaves
½	cup shredded Parmesan cheese	

1. Bring milk and 2 cups water to a boil in a saucepan over medium heat, stirring occasionally. Gradually whisk in grits and salt; return to a boil. Cover, reduce heat to low, and simmer, stirring occasionally, 10 to 15 minutes or until thickened. Remove from heat; stir in cheeses until blended.

2. Layer Texas Smoked Brisket, grits, and Coleslaw in 12 (8-oz.) glasses; drizzle with barbecue sauce. Garnish, if desired. Serve immediately.

COLESLAW

Makes: about 3 cups   Hands-On Time: 10 min.   Total Time: 10 min.

⅓	cup mayonnaise	¼ tsp. salt
2	Tbsp. minced green onions	¼ tsp. freshly ground pepper
1	Tbsp. sugar	1 (10-oz.) package shredded coleslaw mix
2	Tbsp. fresh lemon juice	

1. Whisk together first 6 ingredients in a large bowl. Add coleslaw mix, and toss to coat.

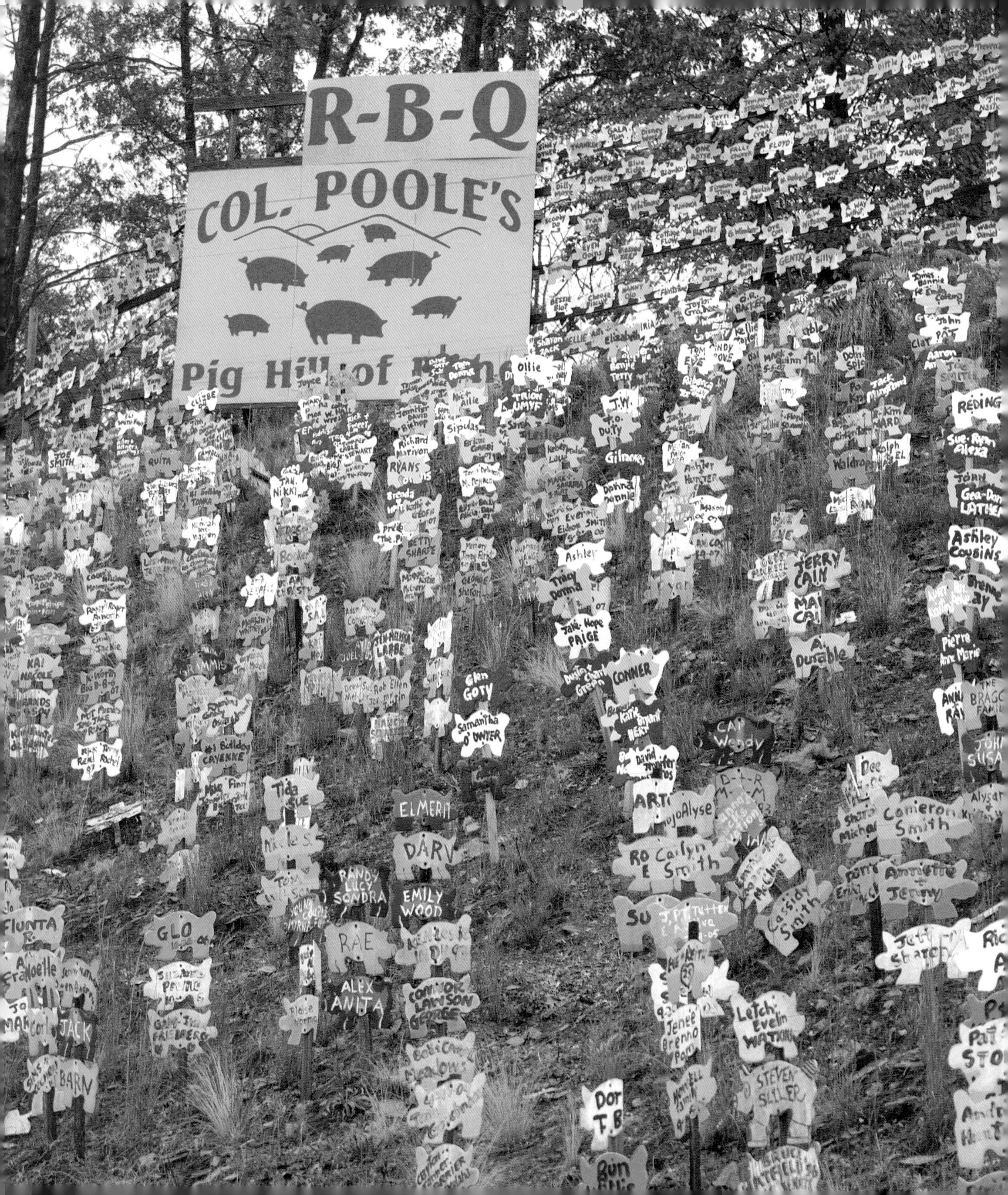
R-B-Q
COL. POOLE'S
Pig Hill of

CANTALOUPE-BACON RELISH

Makes: about 2½ cups   Hands-On Time: 20 min.   Total Time: 20 min.

Serve this relish over salad greens topped with sliced grilled chicken, or try it on grilled crostini with goat cheese as an appetizer.

1½ cups finely diced cantaloupe
½   cup seeded, diced cucumber
5   bacon slices, cooked and crumbled
1   green onion, minced
1   Tbsp. chopped fresh mint

2   Tbsp. extra virgin olive oil
2   to 3 tsp. red wine vinegar
¼   tsp. freshly ground pepper
Pinch of salt

1. Combine all ingredients. Serve immediately.

VIDALIA ONION AND PEACH REFRIGERATOR RELISH

Makes: about 10 (8-oz.) jars   Hands-On Time: 1 hour, 10 min.   Total Time: 3 hours, 25 min.

Take advantage of seasonal fruit and vegetables by sealing in their flavors at their peak. Preserve jars of refrigerator relish for family and friends to enjoy year-round.

2   cups sugar
2   cups cider vinegar
¼   cup gin
2   Tbsp. salt
1   Tbsp. mustard seeds
1   tsp. celery salt

½   tsp. dried crushed red pepper
4   bay leaves, crushed
3   lb. Vidalia onions, finely chopped
3   lb. fresh peaches, peeled and chopped
4   garlic cloves, thinly sliced

1. Bring 2 cups water, sugar, vinegar, gin, salt, mustard seeds, celery salt, dried crushed red pepper, and crushed bay leaves to a boil in a Dutch oven over medium-high heat. Add Vidalia onions, peaches, and garlic; boil, stirring occasionally, 15 minutes. Let mixture cool completely (about 2 hours). Store in airtight containers in refrigerator up to 2 weeks.

"Uniting the nation through barbecue"

Heath Hall

Pork Barrel BBQ
Washington, D.C.

In June of 2008, former United States Senate staffers Heath Hall and Brett Thompson turned their dreams into reality by filling the good barbecue void in the nation's capital. The pair launched their soon-to-be-famous Pork Barrel's All-American Spice Rub and joined forces with others as The Pork Barrel BBQ Competition BBQ Team to compete in the national barbecue circuit.

Heath and Brett have traveled all over the country competing in barbecue cook-offs and championships such as Memphis in May, The American Royal Invitational, and the Jack Daniels World Championships. They have won dozens of awards across many categories—Chicken, Ribs, Pork, and Brisket, and continue to gain applause and recognition for their barbecue sauces. In fact, their sauce was named "Best BBQ Sauce in the Nation" by *Men's Health* magazine.

Between appearances on ABC's *Shark Tank*, and other network news broadcasts, Heath and Brett strive to "unite the nation through the great tradition of barbecue, and bring bipartisan flavor to your next meal."

CHARRED GUACAMOLE WITH GRILLED CORN

Makes: 3¼ cups   Hands-On Time: 23 min.   Total Time: 50 min.

Although this tasty mixture is the perfect sidekick for tortilla chips, it's equally delicious piled on top of south-of-the-border-seasoned grilled chicken or steak.

2	ears fresh corn, husks removed
1	small red onion, cut into ½-inch-thick slices
3	avocados, halved
2	Tbsp. olive oil
1¼	tsp. Pork Barrel BBQ All-American Spice Rub or your favorite spice rub, divided
¼	cup chopped fresh cilantro
¼	cup fresh lime juice
2	garlic cloves, minced

1. Preheat grill to 350° to 400° (medium-high) heat. Brush corn, onion slices, and cut sides of avocados with oil; sprinkle with 1 tsp. rub. Grill corn, covered with grill lid, 12 minutes or until done, turning occasionally. At the same time, grill onion, covered with grill lid, 4 minutes on each side. Grill avocado, cut sides down, covered with grill lid, 3 minutes. Remove from grill; cool 15 minutes.

2. Stir together remaining ¼ tsp. rub, cilantro, lime juice, and garlic in a medium bowl. Hold each ear of corn upright on a cutting board; carefully cut downward, cutting kernels from cob. Add kernels to cilantro mixture in bowl; discard cobs. Chop onion and avocado; add to bowl. Mash mixture with a fork or potato masher just until chunky. Serve immediately.

RECIPE provided by Heath Hall of Pork Barrel BBQ.

MUFFULETTA DIP

Makes: about 4 cups   Hands-On Time: 10 min.   Total Time: 1 hour, 10 min.

Serve this dip with toasted French bread slices or as a topping for grilled chicken or fish.

1 cup Italian olive salad, drained	4 oz. provolone cheese, diced
1 cup diced salami (about 4 oz.)	1 celery rib, finely chopped
¼ cup grated Parmesan cheese	½ red bell pepper, chopped
¼ cup chopped pepperoncini salad peppers	1 Tbsp. olive oil
1 (2¼-oz.) can sliced black olives, drained	¼ cup chopped fresh parsley

1. Stir together first 9 ingredients. Cover and chill 1 to 24 hours before serving. Stir in parsley just before serving. Store leftovers in refrigerator up to 5 days.

NOTE: We tested with Boscoli Italian Olive Salad.

TROY'S TIP

Italian olive salad is a combination of olives and assorted pickled vegetables, like cauliflower and carrots. The vibrant colors of the vegetables and tanginess of the dip provide a tasty enhancement to a variety of grilled meats.

GLAZED BABY BACK RIBS

Makes: 6 servings   Hands-On Time: 42 min.   Total Time: 5 hours, plus 1 day for marinating

2 slabs baby back pork ribs (about 6 lb.)	¼ cup honey
½ cup Pork Dry Rub (page 28)	1 tsp. fresh lemon juice
Hickory wood chips	¼ tsp. ground red pepper
1 cup sweet red barbecue sauce	

1. Remove thin membrane from back of ribs by slicing into it with a knife and then pulling it off. (This will make ribs more tender.) Sprinkle meat generously with Pork Dry Rub. Massage rub into meat. Wrap tightly with plastic wrap, and chill 24 hours.

2. Soak wood chips in water 30 minutes. Prepare a hot fire by piling charcoal on 1 side of grill, leaving other side empty. (For gas grills, light only 1 side.) Place cooking grate on grill. Arrange ribs over unlit side.

3. Cook 2 hours, covered with grill lid, adding 5 to 7 charcoal pieces every 45 minutes to 1 hour, and keeping temperature between 225° and 250°. Add a handful of hickory chips to the charcoal every 20 minutes to 30 minutes. Reposition slabs occasionally, placing the one closest to the heat source in the back and adding hickory chips and coals as needed. Cook 2 more hours. Stir together barbecue sauce, honey, lemon juice, and ground red pepper in a small bowl. Baste ribs generously with barbecue sauce. Cook 15 more minutes. Remove from grill, and let stand 10 minutes.

CHAMPIONSHIP GLAZED RIBS

Makes: 6 servings   Hands-On Time: 40 min.   Total Time: 5 hours

2   slabs pork spare ribs (about 7½ lb.)
1   cup bottled hickory and brown sugar barbecue
     sauce

⅓   cup honey
⅔   cup Pork Dry Rub (page 28)

1. Cut slab perpendicular to the rib bones, reserving rib tips for another use. This style of ribs is known as the St. Louis cut. You can also have your butcher trim them for you.

2. Remove thin membrane from back of ribs by slicing into it with a knife, and then pulling it off. (This will make ribs more tender.)

3. Stir together barbecue sauce and honey in a small bowl; reserve ½ cup to serve with cooked ribs. Sprinkle both sides of ribs generously with Pork Dry Rub; let stand 10 minutes to create a paste.

4. Light 1 side of grill, heating to 250° to 300° (low) heat; leave other side unlit. Place ribs over unlit side, and grill, covered with grill lid, 2 hours and 15 minutes.

5. Turn rib slabs over; grill 2 hours and 15 minutes or until tender. Cook ribs 15 more minutes, basting frequently with barbecue sauce mixture.

6. Remove ribs from grill, and let stand 10 minutes. Cut ribs, slicing between bones. Serve ribs with reserved ½ cup barbecue sauce mixture.

COWBOY NACHOS

Makes: 6 to 8 servings   Hands-On Time: 51 min.   Total Time: 51 min.

Load these nachos with braised brisket and Monterey Jack cheese. Add all of your favorite classic nacho toppings to complete this savory appetizer.

2   (16-oz.) cans seasoned pinto beans, drained
2   tsp. hot sauce
1   tsp. minced garlic
$\frac{1}{2}$ tsp. freshly ground pepper
$3\frac{1}{2}$ cups shredded Texas Smoked Brisket
      (without sauce) (page 42)
1   Tbsp. canola oil

$\frac{1}{2}$ cup taco sauce
$\frac{1}{4}$ cup beef broth
1   (9-oz.) package round tortilla chips
1   (8-oz.) block Monterey Jack cheese, shredded
Pico de Gallo
Toppings: guacamole, sour cream, pickled jalapeño
      pepper slices

1. Preheat oven to 425°. Cook first 4 ingredients and $\frac{1}{2}$ cup water in a medium saucepan, stirring occasionally, over medium-low heat 5 to 7 minutes or until thoroughly heated.

2. Cook brisket in hot oil in a skillet over medium heat, stirring often, 4 minutes or until thoroughly heated. Stir in taco sauce and broth; cook 2 minutes.

3. Divide chips, bean mixture, brisket mixture, cheese, and 1 cup Pico de Gallo among 3 pie plates.

4. Bake at 425° for 5 minutes or until cheese is melted. Serve immediately with remaining Pico de Gallo and desired toppings.

PICO DE GALLO

Makes: $3\frac{1}{2}$ cups   Hands-On Time: 15 min.   Total Time: 15 min.

6   plum tomatoes, chopped
$\frac{1}{2}$ cup finely chopped sweet onion
$\frac{1}{4}$ cup chopped fresh cilantro
1   jalapeño pepper, seeded and minced

2   Tbsp. fresh lime juice
1   garlic clove, minced
$\frac{1}{2}$ tsp. salt

1. Combine all ingredients in a medium bowl. Cover and chill until ready to serve.

NOTE: Nachos can be baked as directed in 2 batches on an aluminum foil-lined baking sheet, topping each batch with 1 cup Pico de Gallo.

CHICKEN-AND-BRISKET BRUNSWICK STEW

Makes: 16 cups   **Hands-On Time: 30 min.**   **Total Time: 2 hours, 40 min.**

2   large onions, chopped
2   garlic cloves, minced
1   Tbsp. vegetable oil
1½ Tbsp. jarred beef soup base
2   lb. skinned and boned chicken breasts
1   (28-oz.) can fire-roasted crushed tomatoes
1   (12-oz.) package frozen white shoepeg or whole kernel corn
1   (10-oz.) package frozen cream-style corn, thawed

1   (9-oz.) package frozen baby lima beans
1   (12-oz.) bottle chili sauce
1   Tbsp. brown sugar
1   Tbsp. yellow mustard
1   Tbsp. Worcestershire sauce
½   tsp. coarsely ground pepper
1   lb. chopped Texas Smoked Brisket (without sauce) (page 42)
1   Tbsp. fresh lemon juice
Hot sauce (optional)

1. Sauté onion and garlic in hot oil in a 7.5-qt. Dutch oven over medium-high heat 3 to 5 minutes or until tender. Combine soup base and 2 cups water; add to Dutch oven. Add chicken and next 9 ingredients. Bring to a boil. Cover, reduce heat to low, and cook, stirring occasionally, 2 hours.

2. Uncover and shred chicken into large pieces using 2 forks. Stir in brisket and lemon juice. Cover and cook 10 minutes. Serve with hot sauce, if desired.

TROY'S TIP

Be sure to shred the chicken while it's still hot. Using forks will prevent you from burning your fingers, and the chicken will easily separate into tender pieces.

"Old-world barbecue made the gourmet way"

Nicole Davenport
Sheffield, TX

As a 4th generation Texas rancher, Nicole Davenport knows a thing or two about good barbecue. She grew up on a ranch outside Sheffield with a Dutch-German mom who was great at making delicious pastries, and a dad who specialized in making sausage and smoking meats.

She combined the two for her Fredericksburg, TX, restaurant, Sugar and Smoke, where folks would come from near and far for homemade sweets and "old world barbecue made the gourmet way." Everything was made from scratch daily with bold Texas flavors and locally sourced ingredients. But the restaurant wasn't the only thing that gave her recognition. Nicole is one of the only female pitmasters who competes in the barbecue circuit. Known as a Wagyu brisket and steak expert, she's appeared on TLC's reality show *BBQ Pitmasters* and Food Network's *Chopped Grill Masters*.

Sugar and Smoke has recently closed so that Nicole can embark upon a new venture in San Antonio—opening Roaring Oak BBQ on Blanco in 2013. She is also working on a cookbook.

SMOKED PAPRIKA PORK ROAST WITH STICKY STOUT BBQ SAUCE

Makes: 8 servings   Hands-On Time: 45 min.   Total Time: 1 hour, 30 min., plus 1 day for chilling

We "dry-brined" the pork before grilling it. This method calls for rubbing a mixture on the pork and chilling it. This allows for salt to pull seasonings into the meat and improve juiciness and flavor. It's unusual, but you do chill uncovered to keep the rub "dry." (Otherwise, the rub dilutes in trapped moisture.)

2   Tbsp. smoked paprika
2   Tbsp. brown sugar
1   Tbsp. kosher salt
1   garlic clove, pressed
1   tsp. coarsely ground pepper

4   tsp. chopped fresh thyme, divided
1   (3½- to 4-lb.) boneless pork loin roast
Kitchen string
Sticky Stout BBQ Sauce

1. Stir together first 5 ingredients and 2 tsp. thyme. Trim pork roast. Rub paprika mixture over pork. Tie roast with kitchen string at 1½-inch intervals, and place in a 13- x 9-inch dish. Chill, uncovered, 24 hours.

2. Light 1 side of grill, heating to 350° to 400° (medium-high) heat; leave other side unlit. Place pork over lit side, and grill, covered with lid, 8 minutes on each side or until browned.

3. Transfer pork to unlit side, and grill, covered with grill lid, 35 to 45 minutes or until a meat thermometer inserted into thickest portion registers 145°. Let stand 10 minutes. Brush with Sticky Stout BBQ Sauce. Sprinkle with remaining 2 tsp. thyme. Serve with remaining sauce.

TROY'S TIP

Mix together the paprika pork rub ingredients a couple hours ahead to allow flavors to blend.

STICKY STOUT BBQ SAUCE

Makes: about 2 cups
Hands-On Time: 15 min.
Total Time: 20 min.

"Sticky" is a Kansas City barbecue (and Asian) term for thick and sweet sauces.

1   **small onion, finely chopped**
1   **Tbsp. vegetable oil**
2   **garlic cloves, minced**
1   **(11.2-oz.) bottle stout beer**
1   **cup spicy barbecue sauce**
¼   **cup fig preserves**
2   **Tbsp. cider vinegar**

1. Sauté onion in hot oil in a large saucepan over medium-high heat 4 to 5 minutes or until tender. Add garlic; sauté 1 minute. Gradually stir in beer. Cook 8 to 10 minutes or until mixture is reduced by half. Reduce heat to medium.

2. Add barbecue sauce and next 2 ingredients, and cook 4 to 5 minutes or until thoroughly heated.

NOTE: Prep and cook sauce 3 days ahead. Cover and chill, and reheat when ready.

HICKORY-SMOKED WHOLE CHICKEN

Makes: 4 to 6 servings   Hands-On Time: 8 min.   Total Time: 4 hours, 53 min.

Whole chickens this large are usually labeled as roasting chickens.

2   cups hickory chips
1   (7- to 7½-lb.) whole chicken
½   cup olive oil

1   cup All-Purpose BBQ Rub (page 29)
White BBQ Sauce (page 23), optional

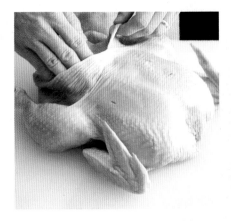
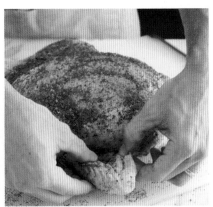

1. Soak wood chips in water 30 minutes. Prepare smoker according to manufacturer's directions, bringing internal temperature to 225° to 250°; maintain temperature for 15 to 20 minutes.

2. Rinse chicken with cold water, and pat dry. Loosen and lift skin from chicken breast and legs with fingers. (Do not totally detach skin.)

3. Rub chicken with oil; rub All-Purpose BBQ Rub under skin on chicken breast and legs and over outside of chicken. Carefully replace skin. Tie ends of legs together with string; tuck wingtips under. Drain wood chips, and place on coals. Place chicken on upper cooking grate; cover with smoker lid. Smoke chicken, maintaining temperature inside smoker between 225° and 250°, for 4½ hours or until a meat thermometer inserted into thickest portion of thigh registers 165°. Add additional charcoal and wood chips as needed. Remove chicken from smoker, and let stand 15 minutes before serving. Serve with White BBQ Sauce, if desired.

DRY-BRINED BEER-CAN CHICKEN

Makes: 8 servings   Hands-On Time: 30 min.   Total Time: 2 hours, plus 1 day for chilling

¼   cup kosher salt
1   Tbsp. light brown sugar
2   tsp. pimentón (sweet smoked Spanish paprika)
1½ tsp. dried marjoram or oregano
1   tsp. dried thyme

1   tsp. freshly ground pepper
3   bay leaves, finely crumbled
2   (3½- to 4-lb.) whole chickens
1   large oven bag
2   (12-oz.) cans brown ale

1. Combine first 7 ingredients in a small bowl. Sprinkle skin and cavities of chickens with salt mixture. Place chickens in oven bag; twist end of bag, and close with tie. Chill 24 hours.

2. Light 1 side of grill, heating to 350° to 400° (medium-high) heat; leave other side unlit. Reserve ½ cup beer from each can for another use. Place each chicken upright onto a beer can, fitting into cavity. Pull legs forward to form a tripod, allowing chickens to stand upright.

3. Place chickens upright on unlit side of grill. Grill, covered with grill lid, 1 hour and 30 minutes to 1 hour and 40 minutes or until golden and a meat thermometer inserted into thickest portion registers 170°. Let stand 10 minutes. Carefully remove chickens from cans; cut into quarters.

SWEET-TEA BRINED CHICKEN

Makes: 6 to 8 servings   Hands-On Time: 1 hour, 35 min.   Total Time: 2 hours, 35 min., plus 1 day for brining

2   family-size tea bags
½   cup firmly packed light brown sugar
¼   cup kosher salt
1   small sweet onion, thinly sliced
1   lemon, thinly sliced

3   garlic cloves, halved
2   (6-inch) fresh rosemary sprigs
1   Tbsp. freshly cracked pepper
2   cups ice cubes
1   (3½- to 4-lb.) cut-up whole chicken

1. Bring 4 cups water to a boil in a 3-qt. heavy saucepan; add tea bags. Remove from heat; cover and steep 10 minutes. Discard tea bags. Stir in sugar and next 6 ingredients, stirring until sugar dissolves. Cool completely (about 45 minutes); stir in ice. (Mixture should be cold before adding chicken.)

2. Place tea mixture and chicken in a large zip-top plastic freezer bag; seal. Place bag in a shallow baking dish, and chill 24 hours. Remove chicken from marinade; discard marinade. Pat chicken dry with paper towels. Light 1 side of grill, heating to 300° to 350° (medium) heat; leave other side unlit.

3. Place chicken, skin side down, over unlit side, and grill, covered with grill lid, 20 minutes. Turn chicken, and grill, covered with grill lid, 40 to 50 minutes or until done. Transfer chicken, skin side down, to lit side of grill, and grill 2 to 3 minutes or until skin is crispy. Let stand 5 minutes before serving.

TROY'S TIP

Brining poultry is a great cooking method you should definitely try. By soaking the meat in a concentrated mixture of salt, water, and seasonings, the brine is absorbed into meat, creating extra moisture that stays locked in and a punch of flavor. Be sure to plan ahead though, as you'll want to soak the meat in the brine for at least 24 hours.

CHICKEN UNDER A SKILLET

Makes: 4 servings   Hands-On Time: 1 hour, 10 min.   Total Time: 2 hours, 15 min.

1 (3- to 4-lb.) whole chicken	1 Tbsp. lemon zest
3 garlic cloves, peeled and quartered	2 Tbsp. fresh lemon juice
1 cup loosely packed fresh flat-leaf parsley leaves	1½ tsp. kosher salt
¼ cup extra virgin olive oil	1½ tsp. herbes de Provence
1 Tbsp. fresh rosemary leaves	1 tsp. freshly ground pepper

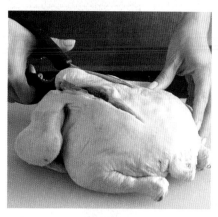 

1. Remove and discard giblets and neck. Rinse chicken, and pat dry. Place chicken, breast side down, on a cutting board. Cut chicken, using kitchen shears, along both sides of backbone, separating backbone from chicken; discard backbone. Open chicken as you would a book. Turn chicken, breast side up, and press firmly against breastbone with the heel of your hand until bone cracks. Tuck wing tips under. Place chicken in a baking dish or pan.

2. Pulse garlic and next 8 ingredients in a food processor until mixture forms a thick paste. Reserve half of paste. Rub remaining paste on both sides of chicken. Cover with plastic wrap, and chill 1 hour.

3. Light 1 side of grill, heating to 300° to 350° (medium) heat; leave other side of grill unlit. Place chicken, breast side down, over lit side of grill; top with a piece of aluminum foil. Place a cast-iron skillet on foil-topped chicken to flatten. Grill, covered with grill lid, 10 to 15 minutes or until chicken is browned. Remove skillet and foil. Turn chicken over, and transfer to unlit side of grill. Grill, covered with grill lid, 45 minutes or until a meat thermometer inserted into thickest portion of breast registers 165°. Remove chicken from grill, and let stand 5 minutes. Brush with reserved paste.

BUTTERMILK-BRINED GRILLED CHICKEN

Makes: 6 servings   Hands-On Time: 20 min.   Total Time: 1 hour, 5 min., plus 1 day for brining

2	cups buttermilk		1	Tbsp. freshly cracked pepper
3	cups cold water		1	small sweet onion, thinly sliced
1/4	cup firmly packed light brown sugar		1	lemon, thinly sliced
1/4	cup hot sauce		3	garlic cloves, halved
3	Tbsp. kosher salt		1	(3½- to 4-lb.) whole cut-up chicken

1. Combine first 6 ingredients in a bowl until sugar is dissolved; stir in onion and next 2 ingredients.

2. Place buttermilk mixture and chicken in a large zip-top plastic freezer bag; seal. Chill 24 hours.

3. Remove chicken from marinade, discarding marinade; pat chicken dry with paper towels.

4. Light 1 side of grill, heating to 300° to 350° (medium) heat. Place chicken, skin side up, over

5. Grill, covered, 40 to 50 minutes or until a meat thermometer inserted into thickest portion

6. Transfer chicken, skin side down to lit side of grill, and grill 2 to 3 minutes or until skin is crispy. Let

GRILLED SWEET GUAVA CHICKEN

Makes: 8 servings   Hands-On Time: 55 min.   Total Time: 9 hours, 35 min.

2   (3½-lb.) whole chickens
2   Tbsp. ground cumin
1   tsp. salt
¼   tsp. freshly ground pepper
½   cup olive oil

⅓   cup fresh lime juice
6   garlic cloves, pressed
Guava Glaze
Garnishes: lemon and lime wedges

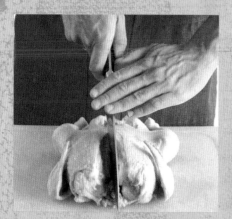

Brush chicken with Guava Glaze. Grill, covered with grill lid, 30 more minutes or until meat thermometer inserted into thickest portion of thigh registers 180° and thickest portion of breast registers 170°, brushing every 10 minutes with glaze. Garnish, if desired.

1. Cut each whole chicken in half, and set aside. Stir together cumin, salt, and pepper in a small bowl. Combine 4 tsp. cumin mixture, olive oil, lime juice, and garlic in a shallow dish or large zip-top plastic freezer bag; reserve remaining cumin mixture. Add chicken to dish or bag; cover or seal, and chill 8 hours or up to 24 hours, turning occasionally.

2. Light 1 side of grill, heating to 400° to 500° (high) heat; leave other side unlit. Remove chicken from marinade; discard marinade. Pat dry with paper towels. Rub reserved cumin mixture over chicken. Arrange, skin side up, on unlit side of grill. Grill, covered with lid, 40 minutes or until a meat thermometer inserted into thickest portion of thigh and breast registers 150°.

TROY'S TIP

Ask your butcher to cut the chickens in half, or substitute chicken breasts and leg quarters.

GUAVA GLAZE

Makes: about ⅔ cup   Hands-On Time: 12 min.   Total Time: 12 min.

¼   cup firmly packed light brown sugar
¼   cup guava jelly

¼   cup apple juice
¼   cup fresh lemon juice

1. Whisk together all ingredients in a small saucepan. Bring to a boil over medium-high heat. Reduce heat to medium-low; simmer 7 minutes or until glaze thickens and reduces slightly, stirring often. Remove from heat; cool.

PAPAW'S SMOKED TURKEY

Makes: 8 to 10 servings   Hands-On Time: 55 min.   Total Time: 8 hours, 10 min., plus 2 days for brining

Brining produces an extra juicy, flavorful turkey breast. It's perfect for sandwiches when thinly sliced.

1   (6- to 6½-lb.) skin-on, bone-in turkey breast
½   cup pickling salt
⅓   cup dark molasses
¼   cup Worcestershire sauce

3   Tbsp. minced garlic
1   Tbsp. freshly ground pepper
Apple wood chips

1. Rinse turkey breast with cold water, and pat dry.

2. Stir together 2 qt. water, salt, and next 4 ingredients in a 2-gal. zip-top plastic freezer bag; add turkey breast. Seal bag, and chill 2 days.

3. Soak wood chips in water 30 minutes. Prepare smoker according to manufacturer's directions,

bringing internal temperature to 225° to 250°, maintaining temperature for 15 to 20 minutes.

4. Remove turkey breast from brine, discarding brine. Rinse under cold running water, and pat dry with paper towels. Drain wood chips, and place on coals. Place turkey breast on lower cooking grate; cover with smoker lid.

5. Smoke turkey breast, maintaining temperature inside smoker between 225° to 250°, for 6½ hours or until a meat thermometer inserted into thickest portion of breast registers 165°. Add additional charcoal and wood chips as needed. Remove turkey from smoker, and let stand 15 minutes before slicing.

PIT STOP

The Salt Lick
Driftwood, TX

Down the road from Austin in Texas Hill Country is this fine gem of a restaurant. They've been smoking brisket, beef and pork ribs, sausages, turkey, and chickens over an open pit since 1967. Thurman Roberts opened the restaurant after family raved over his barbecue at reunions. He and his sons built the barbecue pit, and he would stay Thursday through the weekend until all the meat was sold. Soon, they built a screened porch around the pit, and over the years, the walls expanded to what is known today as The Salt Lick. The current owner, Scott Roberts, is the great-grandson of Bettie Howard who traveled to the area from Desoto, Mississippi, in a chuck wagon. Her method of searing meat and slow cooking over hot coals is still the same method the restaurant uses today.

SMOKED TURKEY-BLUE CHEESE OPEN-FACED SANDWICHES

Makes: 6 servings   **Hands-On Time: 10 min.**   **Total Time: 18 min.**

Fig paste to taste

12   (¼-inch-thick) slices toasted ciabatta or
      French bread

Sliced Papaw's Smoked Turkey (page 79)

1   (8-oz.) round soft-ripened blue-veined Brie

1   cup packed arugula leaves

Pepper to taste

1. Preheat oven to 425°.

2. Spread desired amount of fig paste on toasted bread slices; top with smoked turkey slices and Brie. Place on a parchment paper-lined baking sheet. Bake at 425° for 8 minutes. Remove from oven. Top with arugula and sprinkle with pepper just before serving.

TROY'S TIP

This recipe is a good way to reinvent Papaw's Smoked Turkey. You can also use leftover turkey from Thanksgiving dinner, if you like.

CITRUS-GRILLED TURKEY BREAST

Makes: 6 servings   Hands-On Time: 40 min.   Total Time: 3 hours, 40 min.

1   (5- to 6-lb.) skin-on, bone-in turkey breast
¼   cup chopped fresh flat-leaf parsley
2   garlic cloves, minced
1   Tbsp. lemon zest

2   Tbsp. olive oil
1   tsp. freshly ground pepper
2   tsp. salt, divided

1. Let turkey breast stand at room temperature 30 minutes; rinse with cold water, and pat turkey dry. Stir together parsley, next 4 ingredients, and 1 tsp. salt.

2. Loosen and lift skin from turkey without totally detaching skin, and rub parsley mixture under skin. Replace skin. Sprinkle cavity with ½ tsp. salt; rub into cavity. Sprinkle remaining ½ tsp. salt on skin; rub into skin.

3. Light 1 side of grill, heating to 350° to 400° (medium-high) heat; leave other side unlit. Place turkey over lit side, and grill, without grill lid, 4 minutes on each side or until golden brown. Transfer turkey to unlit side, and grill, covered with grill lid, 2 to 2½ hours or until a meat thermometer inserted into thickest portion registers 165°. Remove from heat, and let stand 30 minutes before slicing.

BEEF IT UP

MARINATED BEEF TENDERLOIN

Makes: 10 to 12 servings   Hands-On Time: 51 min.   Total Time: 9 hours, 6 min.

2   (16-oz.) bottles zesty Italian dressing
⅓   cup soy sauce
⅓   cup dry red wine
1   garlic clove, minced

½   tsp. lemon pepper
1   (5- to 6-lb.) beef tenderloin, trimmed
Horseradish Cream Sauce

1. Stir together first 5 ingredients, and pour into a large shallow dish or zip-top plastic freezer bag; add tenderloin. Cover or seal, and chill 8 hours, turning meat occasionally.

2. Preheat grill to 400° to 500° (high) heat. Remove tenderloin from marinade, discarding marinade.

3. Grill, covered with lid, 24 minutes, turning occasionally. Reduce temperature to medium-low heat (less than 300°); grill, covered with lid, 12 minutes or until a meat thermometer registers 145° (medium-rare) to 160° (medium). Let stand 15 minutes before slicing. Place tenderloin on a serving tray. Serve with Horseradish Cream Sauce.

HORSERADISH CREAM SAUCE

Makes: 1 cup   Hands-On Time: 10 min.   Total Time: 40 min.

1   (8-oz.) container sour cream
2   Tbsp. thinly sliced fresh chives
4   tsp. refrigerated horseradish
1   tsp. lemon zest

½   tsp. coarsely ground pepper
¼   tsp. salt
Garnish: sliced fresh chives

1. Stir together first 6 ingredients in a small bowl. Cover and chill 30 minutes. Garnish, if desired. Store in an airtight container in refrigerator up to 2 days.

GRILLED FILET MIGNON WITH RED WINE MUSHROOM SAUCE

Makes: 4 servings   Hands-On Time: 35 min.   Total Time: 40 min.

Butter and a splash of heavy cream add richness to the sauce that's spooned over these tender filets.

- ⅓ cup butter, divided
- 2 Tbsp. finely chopped shallots
- 1 tsp. minced garlic
- 1 (8-oz.) container sliced baby portobello mushrooms
- ¾ cup dry red wine
- ¼ cup low-sodium fat-free beef broth

- 1 Tbsp. Worcestershire sauce
- 2 tsp. coarse-grained Dijon mustard
- 2 Tbsp. heavy cream
- 4 (8-oz.) beef tenderloin filets (1 inch thick)
- 1 Tbsp. olive oil
- ½ tsp. kosher salt
- ½ tsp. freshly ground pepper

TROY'S TIP

This recipe is wonderful for any special occasion or "just because." The baby portobello mushrooms, sometimes labeled cremini mushrooms, are a great choice to add meatiness and richness to the sauce. Don't season your filets too early; the salt will draw out the moisture and dry them out.

1. Preheat grill to 350° to 400° (medium-high) heat. Melt 1½ Tbsp. butter in a medium saucepan over medium heat. Add shallots and garlic; sauté 2 minutes or until tender. Add mushrooms; sauté 3 minutes or until tender. Stir in wine, broth, Worcestershire sauce, and mustard. Cook 14 to 16 minutes or until liquid is reduced by half.

Stir in cream; cook 1 minute. Add remaining butter, stirring until butter melts. Keep warm.

2. Rub steaks with oil, and sprinkle with salt and pepper. Grill, covered with lid, 8 minutes on each side or to desired degree of doneness. Remove from grill; let stand 5 minutes. Serve with sauce.

GRILLED TRI-TIP WITH CITRUS-CHILE BUTTER

Makes: 8 to 10 servings   **Hands-On Time: 35 min.**   **Total Time: 40 min.**

2   (2-lb.) tri-tip steaks*
2   tsp. salt, divided
1¼ tsp. pepper, divided

Citrus-Chile Butter
3   bunches baby Vidalia or green onions, trimmed
3   Tbsp. olive oil

1. Preheat grill to 350° to 400° (medium-high) heat. Sprinkle steaks with 1½ tsp. salt and 1 tsp. pepper. Grill steaks, covered with grill lid, 9 to 12 minutes on each side or to desired degree of doneness.

2. Remove from grill, and rub

3 Tbsp. Citrus-Chile Butter onto steaks. Cover steaks with aluminum foil; let stand 5 minutes.

3. Meanwhile, toss onions with olive oil; season with remaining ½ tsp. salt and ¼ tsp. pepper. Grill onions, without grill lid, 2 minutes; turn and grill 1 more minute.

4. Uncover steaks, and cut across the grain into thin slices. Serve with grilled onions and remaining Citrus-Chile Butter.

*BEEF STRIP STEAKS (about 2 inches thick) may be substituted.

CITRUS-CHILE BUTTER

Makes: 1 cup   **Hands-On Time: 10 min.**   **Total Time: 10 min.**

1   cup butter, softened
2   Tbsp. lime zest
2   Tbsp. lemon zest
3   garlic cloves, minced

1   Tbsp. seeded and minced jalapeño pepper
1   tsp. chopped fresh thyme
Salt and freshly ground pepper to taste

1. Combine first 6 ingredients. Season with salt and freshly ground pepper to taste.

2. Spoon mixture onto plastic wrap.

3. Shape into a log. Chill until ready to serve, or freeze up to 1 month.

RED WINE TRI-TIP

Makes: 6 to 8 servings   Hands-On Time: 43 min.   Total Time: 48 min., plus 1 day for marinating

This steak gets its delicious flavor from the marinade it soaks in for 24 hours. It's great paired with roasted potatoes.

¾ cup dry red wine
4 garlic cloves, minced
1 small shallot, minced
2 Tbsp. olive oil
2 Tbsp. soy sauce

2 Tbsp. fresh thyme leaves
1½ tsp. kosher salt, divided
1½ tsp. freshly ground pepper, divided
2 (1¾-lb.) tri-tip roasts
2 Tbsp. butter

1. Combine first 6 ingredients, 1 tsp. salt, and 1 tsp. pepper in a large shallow dish or zip-top plastic freezer bag; add roasts, turning to coat. Cover or seal, and chill 24 hours, turning once.

2. Preheat grill to 350° to 400° (medium-high) heat. Remove roasts from marinade, reserving marinade. Pat roasts dry; sprinkle with remaining ½ tsp. salt and ½ tsp. pepper. Grill, covered with grill lid, 2 minutes on each side. Reduce grill to medium heat. Grill, covered with grill lid, 12 minutes on each side or to desired degree of doneness. Remove from grill; let stand 5 minutes. Cut roasts across the grain into thin slices.

3. Bring reserved marinade to a boil in a saucepan over medium-high heat. Reduce heat, and simmer, uncovered, 8 minutes or until reduced by about half; skim off foam with a spoon, if necessary. Remove from heat; add butter, stirring to melt. Serve sauce with roast.

TROY'S TIP

The tri-tip roast comes from the bottom of the sirloin and is often labeled as tri-tip steak or triangle roast.

BLUE CHEESE-ENCRUSTED STRIP STEAKS

Makes: 4 servings   Hands-On Time: 22 min.   Total Time: 22 min.

Soft, fresh breadcrumbs and moist blue cheese crumbled straight from the block are the secrets to a flavorful topping for the steaks.

½   cup crumbled blue cheese

¼   cup soft, fresh breadcrumbs

1   tsp. chopped fresh parsley

1   tsp. finely chopped shallots

3   garlic cloves, minced

4   (12-oz.) beef strip steaks (1½ inches thick)

2   Tbsp. olive oil

½   tsp. kosher salt

½   tsp. freshly ground pepper

1. Preheat grill to 350° to 400° (medium-high) heat. Toss together first 5 ingredients in a medium bowl. Rub steaks with oil, and sprinkle with salt and pepper.

2. Grill steaks, covered with lid, 3 minutes on each side. Remove steaks from grill; top with cheese mixture. Return to grill; grill, covered with lid, 3 more minutes or to desired degree of doneness and topping is browned.

TROY'S TIP

Soft breadcrumbs can be made with leftover bakery rolls so nothing goes to waste.

VIETNAMESE BBQ TACOS

Makes: 8 servings   Hands-On Time: 30 min.   Total Time: 8 hours, 50 min., including sauce

3   beef strip steaks (about 2½ lb.)
¼   cup fish sauce
¼   cup rice wine vinegar
2   Tbsp. grated fresh ginger
3   garlic cloves, minced
2   Tbsp. sugar
2   Tbsp. honey
1   Tbsp. sesame oil

1   tsp. freshly ground pepper
½   medium-size red onion, sliced
8   (8-inch) soft taco-size flour tortillas, warmed
Vietnamese Dipping Sauce
Toppings: thinly sliced red cabbage, matchstick
        carrots, thinly sliced red onion, chopped
        fresh cilantro, chopped fresh mint,
        cucumber slices

1. Place steaks in a large zip-top plastic freezer bag. Whisk together fish sauce and next 7 ingredients. Stir in red onion, and pour mixture over steaks in freezer bag. Seal and chill 8 to 24 hours, turning once.

2. Preheat grill to 350° to 400° (medium-high) heat. Remove steaks from marinade, discarding marinade. Grill steaks 7 to 8 minutes on each side or to desired degree of doneness, turning every 3 to 5 minutes.

3. Cover loosely with aluminum foil, and let stand 10 minutes. Cut steaks across the grain into thin strips, and serve in warm flour tortillas with Vietnamese Dipping Sauce and desired toppings.

VIETNAMESE DIPPING SAUCE

Makes: 1 cup   Hands-On Time: 10 min.   Total Time: 10 min.

¼   cup fish sauce
¼   cup white vinegar
3   Tbsp. sugar
2   Tbsp. fresh lime juice

2   garlic cloves, minced
1   serrano pepper or Thai chile pepper, seeded
     and sliced

1. Stir together ½ cup water, fish sauce, vinegar, sugar, lime juice, garlic, and serrano pepper in a medium bowl. Store in an airtight container in refrigerator up to 1 week.

BEER-AND-BROWN SUGAR RIB-EYES

Makes: 4 servings   Hands-On Time: 12 min.   Total Time: 17 min., plus 1 day for marinating

Your favorite dark beer, teriyaki sauce, and brown sugar create a simple yet flavorful marinade for juicy rib-eye steaks.

½   cup dark beer
¼   cup teriyaki marinade and sauce
¼   cup firmly packed brown sugar

4   (1-inch-thick) rib-eye steaks (about 3 lb.)
¾   tsp. kosher salt
¾   tsp. freshly ground pepper

1. Whisk together first 3 ingredients in a large shallow dish or zip-top plastic freezer bag.

2. Add steaks, turning to coat. Cover or seal, and chill 24 hours, turning once.

3. Preheat grill to 350° to 400° (medium-high) heat. Remove steaks from marinade, discarding marinade. Sprinkle steaks with salt and pepper. Grill, covered with grill lid, 5 minutes on each side or to desired degree of doneness. Remove from grill, and let stand 5 minutes.

CURRIED BEEF KABOBS WITH JADE SAUCE

Makes: 12 servings   Hands-On Time: 20 min.   Total Time: 50 min.

12   (6-inch) wooden skewers
2   Tbsp. peanut oil
1¼ tsp. garam masala
1¼ tsp. freshly ground roasted garlic and sea salt
¾   tsp. curry powder

½   tsp. freshly ground mixed peppercorns
¼   tsp. ground cumin
1½ lb. flat-iron steak, cut into 1-inch pieces
Jade Sauce
½   cup sweetened flaked coconut, toasted

1. Soak wooden skewers in water 30 minutes.

2. Preheat grill to 350° to 400° (medium-high) heat. Whisk together peanut oil and next 5 ingredients in a large bowl until blended. Add steak pieces, and toss to coat. Thread beef onto skewers.

3. Grill beef, covered with grill lid, 3 minutes on each side or to desired degree of doneness.

4. Place skewers on a serving platter, and drizzle with Jade Sauce. Sprinkle with toasted flaked coconut.

JADE SAUCE

Makes: ⅔ cup   Hands-On Time: 5 min.   Total Time: 5 min.

½   cup chopped fresh cilantro
¼   cup chopped fresh mint
¼   cup extra virgin olive oil
2   Tbsp. chopped green onions
1   tsp. grated lime zest

1   Tbsp. fresh lime juice
2   tsp. seeded and minced jalapeño pepper
2   tsp. honey
1   tsp. minced garlic
¼   tsp. salt

1. Process all ingredients in a food processor 10 seconds or until thoroughly blended, stopping to scrape down sides as needed.

MEXICAN GRILLED SKIRT STEAK

Makes: 4 servings   **Hands-On Time: 20 min.**   **Total Time: 25 min., plus 1 day for marinating**

Slice the steak thinly, and serve it with grilled peppers and onions rolled in flour tortillas.

3   garlic cloves
¾   tsp. kosher salt
1½ tsp. olive oil
¾   tsp. paprika
¾   tsp. ground cumin

¾   tsp. ground coriander
½   tsp. freshly ground pepper
½   tsp. ground cinnamon
1¼ lb. skirt steak

1. Mince garlic with kosher salt to create a paste. Stir together garlic mixture, oil, and next 5 ingredients in a small bowl.

2. Pat steak dry with paper towels. Rub paste over steak. Cover and chill 24 hours. Preheat grill to 350° to 400° (medium-high) heat.

3. Grill steak, without grill lid, 2 minutes on each side or to desired degree of doneness. Let stand 5 minutes. Cut steak across the grain into thin slices.

FLANK STEAK SANDWICHES WITH APPLE BBQ SAUCE

Makes: 6 servings   Hands-On Time: 25 min.   Total Time: 8 hours, 25 min.

1   (1½-lb.) flank steak
Apple BBQ Sauce
6   onion rolls, split
6   tomato slices

6   lettuce leaves
Red onion slices (optional)
Coarsely ground pepper

1. Place steak in a shallow dish or zip-top plastic freezer bag; pour ½ cup Apple BBQ Sauce over steak. Cover or seal, and chill 8 hours, turning meat occasionally.

2. Preheat grill to 350° to 400° (medium-high) heat. Remove steak from marinade, discarding marinade. Grill steak, covered with grill lid, 7 minutes on each side or to desired degree of doneness.

3. Cut steak diagonally across the grain into thin strips. Serve on rolls with tomato, lettuce, and, if desired, onion. Drizzle with remaining sauce; sprinkle with pepper.

APPLE BBQ SAUCE

Makes: 1⅓ cups   Hands-On Time: 25 min.   Total Time: 25 min.

½   cup apple jelly
1   (8-oz.) can no-salt-added tomato sauce
¼   cup white vinegar

2   Tbsp. light brown sugar
1   tsp. hot sauce
¼   tsp. salt

1. Combine jelly, tomato sauce, vinegar, sugar, 2 Tbsp. water, hot sauce and salt in a small saucepan. Bring to a boil over medium-high heat, stirring until smooth. Reduce heat, and simmer, stirring occasionally, 20 to 25 minutes.

BALSAMIC-MARINATED FLAT-IRON STEAK

Makes: 4 servings   Hands-On Time: 9 min.   Total Time: 8 hours, 29 min.

Marinating the steak 8 hours ahead gets the prep out of the way and makes for a dinner that's quick and easy to get on the table.

½   cup olive oil
¼   cup balsamic vinegar
1   Tbsp. whole grain mustard
2   Tbsp. soy sauce

2   Tbsp. honey
2   garlic cloves, minced
1½ lb. flat-iron steaks

1. Combine first 6 ingredients in a large dish or zip-top plastic freezer bag; add steaks, turning to coat. Cover or seal, and chill 8 to 24 hours, turning once.

2. Preheat grill to 350° to 400° (medium-high) heat. Remove steaks from marinade, discarding marinade.

3. Grill steaks, covered with grill lid, 7 minutes on each side or to desired degree of doneness. Let stand 5 minutes. Cut steaks across the grain into thin slices.

TROY'S TIP

Flat-iron steak is now readily available at most groceries. It's a great flavorful cut from the chuck and is sometimes labeled as top blade roast.

LEMON FLANK STEAK SKEWERS

Makes: 12 to 16 appetizer servings **Hands-On Time: 33 min.** **Total Time: 8 hours, 43 min.**

4 (2-lb.) flank steaks
⅔ cup olive oil
4 tsp. lemon zest
½ cup fresh lemon juice
2 tsp. salt

½ tsp. dried crushed red pepper
50 (12-inch) wooden skewers
Lemon Dipping Sauce
Garnish: lemon wedges

TROY'S TIP

Flank steak is such a great cut of beef, but you need to be sure to cut it thinly across the grain so it's not tough. For this recipe, freeze the flank steak for 10 minutes to make slicing easier.

1. Cut steaks diagonally into ¼-inch slices. Combine olive oil and next 4 ingredients in a shallow dish or zip-top plastic freezer bag; add steak. Cover or seal, and chill 8 hours, turning occasionally.

2. Soak wooden skewers in water 30 minutes.

3. Preheat grill to 350° to 400° (medium-high) heat. Remove steak from marinade, discarding marinade. Thread each steak slice onto 1 skewer.

4. Grill beef, covered with grill lid, 4 to 5 minutes on each side or to desired degree of doneness. Serve with Lemon Dipping Sauce. Garnish, if desired.

LEMON DIPPING SAUCE

Makes: 4½ cups **Hands-On Time: 10 min.** **Total Time: 1 hour, 10 min.**

One medium lemon yields 2 to 3 Tbsp. lemon juice and 1½ to 2 tsp. lemon zest.

2 (16-oz.) containers reduced-fat sour cream
2 Tbsp. refrigerated horseradish
2 tsp. lemon zest

6 Tbsp. fresh lemon juice
1 tsp. salt
Garnish: lemon zest

1. Combine first 5 ingredients; cover and chill at least 1 hour. Garnish, if desired.

GRILLED MOLASSES FLANK STEAK WITH WATERMELON SALSA

Makes: 6 to 8 servings   **Hands-On Time: 30 min.**   **Total Time: 5 hours, 25 min.**

Smoky-sweet molasses infuses the steak with flavor while a fruit salsa adds a crisp, cooling accent.

³/₄   **cup molasses**
¹/₃   **cup soy sauce**
¹/₄   **cup canola oil**
¹/₄   **cup fresh lemon juice**
2   **Tbsp. Worcestershire sauce**
2   **Tbsp. grated fresh ginger**

3   **garlic cloves, minced**
1   **tsp. dried crushed red pepper**
1   **(2-lb.) flank steak**
Salt and pepper to taste
Watermelon Salsa

1. Place first 8 ingredients in a 2-gal. zip-top plastic freezer bag; squeeze bag to combine. Add steak; seal bag, and chill 4 to 12 hours. Remove steak from marinade, discarding marinade.

2. Preheat grill to 400° to 450° (high) heat. Grill steak, covered with grill lid, 9 minutes on each side or to desired degree of doneness. Remove from grill, and let stand 10 minutes. Cut diagonally across the grain into thin slices. Season with salt and pepper to taste. Top with Watermelon Salsa.

WATERMELON SALSA

Makes: about 4 cups   **Hands-On Time: 20 min.**   **Total Time: 35 min.**

This colorful salsa makes a delicious topping for sliced tomatoes, grilled chicken, or steak.

1   **cup diced unpeeled nectarine**
2   **jalapeño peppers, seeded and minced**
1   **Tbsp. sugar**
3   **Tbsp. fresh lime juice**
2   **tsp. orange zest**

2   **tsp. grated fresh ginger**
2   **cups seeded and diced watermelon**
¹/₂   **cup chopped fresh cilantro**
¹/₃   **cup diced red onion**

1. Stir together first 6 ingredients in a large bowl; let stand 15 minutes. Add watermelon and next 2 ingredients, and toss gently to coat. Serve immediately, or cover and chill up to 24 hours.

LIME-CILANTRO FLANK STEAK

Makes: 8 servings   **Hands-On Time: 26 min.**   **Total Time: 8 hours, 31 min.**

Leaving the seeds in the jalapeño imparts a flavor kick without being too fiery.

1   cup fresh lime juice (8 limes)
½   cup chopped red onion
½   cup chopped fresh cilantro
3   Tbsp. brown sugar
2   Tbsp. vegetable oil

2   tsp. kosher salt
½   tsp. freshly ground pepper
8   garlic cloves, minced
1   jalapeño pepper, halved
2   (2-lb.) flank steaks

1. Process all ingredients except steaks in a food processor until puréed, stopping to scrape down sides as needed. Pour mixture into a large shallow dish or zip-top plastic freezer bag; add steaks, turning to coat. Cover or seal, and chill 8 hours, turning once.

2. Preheat grill to 350° to 400° (medium-high) heat. Remove steaks from marinade, discarding marinade. Grill steaks, covered with grill lid, 5 minutes on each side or to desired degree of doneness. Remove from grill, and let stand 5 minutes. Cut steaks diagonally across the grain into thin slices.

TROY'S TIP

It's important to stick to the marinate time for this recipe. The acidic lime juice works as a tenderizer up to 8 hours, but longer than that and it'll actually begin to cook the meat proteins and make it tough.

ROSEMARY FLANK STEAK WITH FIG SALSA

Makes: 6 servings   Hands-On Time: 30 min.   Total Time: 1 hour, 5 min.

1	Tbsp. chopped fresh rosemary		3	cups chopped fresh figs
2	garlic cloves, minced		1	green onion, minced
¾	tsp. kosher salt		2	Tbsp. chopped fresh parsley
½	tsp. freshly ground pepper		2	Tbsp. seasoned rice wine vinegar
3	Tbsp. olive oil, divided			Salt and pepper to taste
1	(1¼-lb.) flank steak		3	oz. Gorgonzola cheese, crumbled

1. Stir together first 4 ingredients and 1 Tbsp. olive oil. Rub onto steak; cover and chill 30 minutes to 4 hours.

2. Preheat grill to 400° to 450° (high) heat. Toss together figs, next 3 ingredients, and remaining 2 Tbsp. oil. Season with salt and pepper to taste.

3. Grill steak, covered with grill lid, 5 minutes on each side or to desired degree of doneness. Let stand 5 minutes.

4. Cut steak diagonally across the grain into thin strips, and arrange on a serving platter. Spoon fig salsa over steak, and sprinkle with Gorgonzola.

STEAK-AND-BLUE CHEESE POTATO SALAD

Makes: 6 servings   Hands-On Time: 25 min.   Total Time: 35 min.

1   lb. asparagus
1½   lb. baby yellow potatoes, halved
2   Tbsp. olive oil
1   (1½-lb.) flank steak
1   tsp. freshly ground pepper
½   tsp. salt
1   red bell pepper, cut into fourths
1   red onion, cut into 8 wedges

½   cup red wine vinegar
⅓   cup olive oil
1   Tbsp. coarse-grained mustard
1   tsp. lemon zest
3   Tbsp. lemon juice
1   garlic clove, pressed
1   tsp. salt
1   (4-oz.) wedge blue cheese, crumbled

1. Preheat grill to 350° to 400° (medium-high) heat. Snap off and discard tough ends of asparagus. Place potatoes in a single layer in center of a large piece of heavy-duty aluminum foil, and drizzle with 2 Tbsp. olive oil. Bring up sides over potatoes; double fold top and side edges to seal, making a packet. Sprinkle steak with ground pepper and ½ tsp. salt. Grill steak, potatoes (in foil packet), asparagus, bell pepper, and onion at same time, covered with grill lid. Grill potatoes and steak 7 to 8 minutes on each side or until steak is desired degree of doneness and potatoes are done,

using tongs to shake foil packet just before turning. Grill asparagus, bell pepper, and onion 4 to 5 minutes or until tender. Let steak and vegetables stand 10 minutes.

2. Meanwhile, whisk together vinegar and next 6 ingredients in a small bowl. Place potatoes in a large bowl; toss with half of vinegar mixture, reserving remaining vinegar mixture. Cut steak diagonally across the grain into thin strips. Toss together steak, potatoes, and grilled vegetables, and top with blue cheese. Drizzle with reserved vinegar mixture.

PIT STOP

Full Moon Bar-B-Que
Birmingham, AL

Back in 1981, former University of Alabama assistant football coach Pat James and his wife, Eloise, opened up the "Best Little Pork House in Alabama." What was then known as Pat James' Full Moon Bar-B-Que is now owned by brothers David and Joe Maluff. The two bought the place in 1996 and have continued to use the same methods of cooking pork, chicken, and beef low and slow over a hickory wood fire pit and slathering on Full Moon's own barbecue sauce. They've got everything from chopped barbecue to fall-off-the-bone ribs and all the fixin's like onion rings and baked beans. Must-orders are the vinegar coleslaw, chow-chow, and half moon cookies.

PINEAPPLE-JALAPEÑO BURGERS

Makes: 6 servings   Hands-On Time: 28 min.   Total Time: 28 min.

Let ground beef stand at room temperature for 10 minutes before grilling.

lb. ground sirloin	6 (¼-inch-thick) pineapple slices
lb. ground chuck	Hamburger buns
tsp. salt	Cilantro-Jalapeño Cream
/₂ tsp. freshly ground pepper	Toppings: avocado slices, fresh cilantro sprigs,
/₃ cup pickled sliced jalapeño peppers, minced	diced red onion

. Preheat grill to 350° to 400° (medium-high) heat. Combine first 4 ingredients gently. Stir minced jalapeño peppers into meat mixture.

. Shape mixture into 6 (5-inch) patties.

3. Grill, covered with grill lid, 4 to 5 minutes on each side or until beef is no longer pink in center. Grill pineapple over medium-high heat 1 to 2 minutes on each side. Serve burgers on buns. Top each burger with Cilantro-Jalapeño Cream, grilled pineapple, avocado slices, a cilantro sprig, and diced red onion.

CILANTRO-JALAPEÑO CREAM

Makes: ¾ cup   Hands-On Time: 10 min.   Total Time: 40 min.

/₂ cup sour cream	1 medium jalapeño pepper, seeded and minced
/₄ cup chopped fresh cilantro	2 Tbsp. fresh lime juice

. Combine all ingredients, and let stand at room temperature 30 minutes. To make ahead, store mixture in an

GORGONZOLA-STUFFED HAMBURGERS

Makes: 4 servings   Hands-On Time: 22 min.   Total Time: 52 min.

Chilling the stuffed patties before grilling not only provides a great make-ahead bonus, but it also firms the cheese and the patties so the stuffing stays inside and not on the grill.

1	(8-oz.) package sliced fresh mushrooms
2	Tbsp. butter, melted
¼	tsp. salt
⅛	tsp. coarsely ground pepper
2	oz. cream cheese, softened
2	Tbsp. crumbled Gorgonzola cheese

1	Tbsp. grated onion
1	Tbsp. Dijon mustard
1½	lb. ground round
¾	tsp. coarsely ground pepper
½	tsp. salt

1. Preheat grill to 350° to 400° (medium-high) heat. Cut an 18- x 12-inch sheet of heavy-duty aluminum foil. Place mushrooms in center of foil. Drizzle with butter; sprinkle with ¼ tsp. salt and ⅛ tsp. pepper. Gather edges of foil to form a pouch; tightly seal edges.

2. Stir together cream cheese and next 3 ingredients in a small bowl. Combine ground round, ¾ tsp. pepper, and ½ tsp. salt in a large bowl until blended. (Do not overwork meat mixture.) Shape mixture into 8 (4-inch) patties; spoon cheese mixture evenly into center of each of 4 patties. Top with remaining 4 patties, pressing edges to seal. Cover and chill 30 minutes.

3. Grill patties, covered with grill lid, 6 to 7 minutes on each side or until done. At the same time, grill mushrooms in foil packet, covered with grill lid, 10 minutes or until tender, turning once. Top hamburgers with mushroom mixture.

HOG
★ SINCE ★ 1986 ★
HEAVEN
A MUSIC CITY ORIGINAL

PIG OUT

APPLE-KALE STUFFED PORK LOIN

Makes: 8 to 10 servings
Hands-On Time: 25 min.
Total Time: 10 hours, 5 min.

Grilling the meat over indirect heat ensures a moist interior.

- (3½-lb.) boneless pork loin
- ¼ cup firmly packed light brown sugar
- ¼ cup yellow mustard
- ¼ cup red wine vinegar
- 2 Tbsp. All-Purpose BBQ Rub (page 29)
- 2 Tbsp. canola oil
- tsp. salt, divided
- tsp. freshly ground pepper, divided
- 6 bacon slices
- Granny Smith apple, peeled and chopped
- small onion, chopped
- 3 cups chopped fresh kale
- 2 Tbsp. cider vinegar
- Kitchen string

1. Butterfly pork loin by making a horizontal cut (about one-third down from top) into 1 side of pork, cutting to within ½ inch of other side. (Do not cut all the way through roast.) Unfold top cut piece, open, and lay flat. Butterfly and repeat procedure on opposite side of remaining two-thirds portion of pork loin, beginning at top or bottom of inside cut.

2. Place pork between 2 sheets of heavy-duty plastic wrap, and flatten to 1-inch thickness, using a rolling pin or flat side of meat mallet. Whisk together brown sugar and next 4 ingredients in a small bowl until well blended. Pour marinade into a large shallow dish or zip-top plastic freezer bag; add pork, turning to coat. Cover or seal, and chill 8 to 24 hours, turning occasionally.

3. Remove pork from marinade, discarding marinade. Lay pork flat on work surface; sprinkle with ½ tsp. salt and ½ tsp. pepper. Light 1 side of grill, heating to 350° to 400° (medium-high) heat; leave other side unlit. Cook bacon in a large skillet over medium-high heat 5 minutes or until crisp; remove bacon, and drain on paper towels, reserving 2 Tbsp. drippings in skillet. Crumble bacon.

4. Sauté apple, onion, and kale in hot drippings 10 minutes or until tender. Add vinegar, stirring to loosen particles from bottom of skillet. Remove from heat; stir in bacon and remaining salt and pepper. Spread kale mixture over pork, leaving a ½-inch border.

5. Roll up, starting at 1 long side, and tie with kitchen string, securing at 2-inch intervals. Place over lit side, and grill, covered with lid, 5 minutes on each side or until browned. Transfer roast to unlit side; grill, covered with lid, 1 hour and 30 minutes or until a meat thermometer registers 145°. Remove from grill;

EDLEYS

Bar-B-Que

"A Tribute to All

Things Southern"

GIFT CARDS

EDLEY'S
BAR-B-QUE

Edleys Bar-B-Que

MAPLE-AND-MUSTARD PORK LOIN

Makes: 10 to 12 servings   Hands-On Time: 50 min.   Total Time: 55 min.

1   (4¾-lb.) boneless pork loin
3   Tbsp. olive oil
½   tsp. salt
¼   tsp. freshly ground pepper
1   cup maple syrup

⅓   cup Dijon mustard
3   Tbsp. cider vinegar
3   Tbsp. soy sauce
Pinch of salt
Pinch of freshly ground pepper

1. Preheat grill to 300° to 350° (medium) heat. Rub pork loin with oil, and sprinkle with ½ tsp. salt and ¼ tsp. pepper.

2. Stir together maple syrup and next 5 ingredients in a small bowl; reserve ½ cup syrup mixture to serve with cooked pork.

3. Grill pork, covered with grill lid, 45 minutes or until a meat thermometer inserted into thickest portion registers 145°, turning every 10 minutes and basting with remaining syrup mixture. Remove from grill, and let stand 5 minutes before slicing. Serve with reserved ½ cup syrup mixture.

TROY'S TIP

Allowing the roast to stand at least 5 minutes after cooking and before slicing ensures that the juices will redistribute instead of escaping once the meat is cut.

ITALIAN GRILLED PORK SANDWICHES

Makes: 6 servings
Hands-On Time: 25 min.
Total Time: 3 hours, 58 min.

2   Tbsp. minced garlic,
     divided
1½   Tbsp. finely chopped fresh
     rosemary
7   Tbsp. extra virgin olive oil,
     divided
1   Tbsp. kosher salt
2   tsp. freshly ground black
     pepper
1   (2¾-lb.) boneless pork loin
1   bunch broccoli rabe
½   tsp. dried crushed red
     pepper
12   (0.6-oz.) smoked provolone
     cheese slices
6   hoagie rolls, split

1. Stir together 1½ Tbsp. garlic, rosemary, 3 Tbsp. oil, salt, and pepper in a small bowl. Place pork in a baking dish; rub pork with garlic mixture. Cover and chill at least 2 hours. Let pork stand at room temperature 45 minutes.

2. Meanwhile, light 1 side of grill, heating to 350° to 400° (medium-high) heat; leave other side unlit. Place pork over lit side, and grill, covered with grill lid, 4 minutes, turning often.

4. Remove florets from broccoli rabe. Trim and discard ½ inch of stem from bottom of broccoli rabe. Cook leaves and stems in boiling water 2 minutes. Add florets; cook 5 minutes.

5. Drain, reserving ½ cup cooking water, and plunge into an ice-water bath. Heat remaining 4 Tbsp. oil in a large skillet over medium heat.

3. Transfer pork to unlit side of grill, and grill, covered with grill lid, 30 minutes or until a meat thermometer inserted into thickest portion registers 145°. Remove from grill, and let stand 5 minutes before slicing.

6. Add remaining garlic and red pepper; sauté 1 minute. Add broccoli; sauté 5 minutes. Add reserved ½ cup water; cook 2 more minutes. Arrange 2 cheese slices on bottom halves of rolls; top with pork, broccoli, and tops of rolls.

RECIPE provided by Heath Hall of Pork Barrel BBQ.

WHISKEY-MARINATED PORK TENDERLOIN

Makes: 4 servings   **Hands-On Time: 25 min.**   **Total Time: 2 hours, 35 min.**

Pork tenderloin should be served slightly pink in the center, so check the time closely. It shouldn't take more than 16 to 18 minutes to reach 145°; then cover the pork, and let it stand while you boil the marinade to serve as a sauce.

1	(1-lb.) pork tenderloin
6	Tbsp. Worcestershire sauce
3	Tbsp. bourbon or whiskey
3	Tbsp. maple syrup
2	Tbsp. honey-Dijon mustard
2	Tbsp. olive oil
¼	tsp. freshly ground pepper
½	tsp. salt

1. Remove silver skin from tenderloin, leaving a thin layer of fat.

2. Whisk together Worcestershire sauce and next 5 ingredients in a small bowl until blended. Pour marinade into a large shallow dish or zip-top plastic freezer bag; add pork, cover or seal, and chill 2 hours, turning occasionally. Remove pork, reserving marinade. Sprinkle pork with salt.

3. Preheat grill to 350° to 400° (medium-high) heat. Grill tenderloin, covered with grill lid, 8 to 9 minutes on each side or until a meat thermometer inserted into thickest portion registers 145°. Remove from grill, and let stand 10 minutes before slicing.

4. Meanwhile, bring reserved marinade to a boil in a small saucepan over medium-high heat. Boil, stirring occasionally, 2 minutes. Serve with sliced pork.

TROY'S TIP

Serve this pork tenderloin with mashed potatoes, using the sauce as "gravy" over the potatoes.

SWEET-AND-SOUR PORK TENDERLOIN

Makes: 4 servings   Hands-On Time: 39 min.   Total Time: 44 min.

Be sure to wear gloves when seeding and mincing jalapeño peppers. The compound in chiles (called capsaicin) that makes them taste spicy will also burn your fingers.

2 Tbsp. sugar	½ tsp. salt
6 Tbsp. cider vinegar	1½ tsp. minced fresh ginger
2 Tbsp. ketchup	1 lb. pork tenderloin
2 Tbsp. molasses	1 Tbsp. olive oil
1 Tbsp. minced garlic	½ tsp. kosher salt
1 Tbsp. seeded and minced jalapeño pepper	½ tsp. coarsely ground black pepper

1. Whisk together first 8 ingredients in a small saucepan; bring to a boil. Remove from heat, and cool 30 minutes. Reserve ¼ cup sauce to serve with cooked pork.

2. Preheat grill to 300° to 350° (medium) heat. Remove silver skin from tenderloin, leaving a thin layer of fat. Rub pork tenderloin with oil; sprinkle with salt and pepper.

3. Grill pork, covered with grill lid, 18 minutes, turning occasionally, or until a meat thermometer inserted into thickest portion registers 145°, basting often with remaining ½ cup sauce. Remove from grill, and let stand 5 minutes before slicing. Slice and serve with reserved ¼ cup sauce.

BOURBON-BROWN SUGAR PORK TENDERLOIN

Makes: 6 to 8 servings   Hands-On Time: 45 min.   Total Time: 45 min., plus 8 hours for marinating

2   (1-lb.) pork tenderloins*
¼   cup firmly packed dark brown sugar
¼   cup minced green onions
¼   cup bourbon

¼   cup soy sauce
¼   cup Dijon mustard
½   tsp. freshly ground pepper
½   tsp. cornstarch

1. Remove silver skin from tenderloins, leaving a thin layer of fat. Combine brown sugar and next 5 ingredients in a large zip-top plastic freezer bag; add pork. Seal bag, and chill 8 to 18 hours, turning bag occasionally. Remove pork from marinade, reserving marinade.

2. Preheat grill to 350° to 400° (medium-high) heat. Grill pork, covered with grill lid, 8 minutes on each side or until a meat thermometer inserted into thickest portion registers 155°. Remove from grill, and let stand 10 minutes.

3. Meanwhile, combine reserved marinade and cornstarch in a saucepan. Bring to a boil over medium heat; cook, stirring constantly, 1 minute. Cut pork diagonally into thin slices, and arrange on a serving platter; drizzle with warm sauce.

*FLANK STEAK (1½ lb.) may be substituted. Reduce grill time to 6 to 8 minutes on each side or to desired degree of doneness.

PORK TENDERLOIN SLIDERS WITH SPICY PICKLES

Makes: 16 servings   **Hands-On Time:** 21 min.   **Total Time:** 26 min., plus 1 day for marinating

The special marinated pickles on these sliders will make these sandwiches a hit at your next backyard cookout.

1 (16-oz.) jar dill pickle chips, drained	2 Tbsp. olive oil
¼ cup sugar	1½ tsp. kosher salt
2 tsp. chipotle hot sauce	½ tsp. freshly ground pepper
½ tsp. dried crushed red pepper	½ cup bottled sweet red barbecue sauce, divided
2 (1-lb.) pork tenderloins	16 yeast rolls, split

1. Stir together first 4 ingredients in a large bowl or zip-top plastic freezer bag; cover or seal, and chill 24 hours.

2. Preheat grill to 300° to 350° (medium) heat. Rub tenderloins with olive oil, and sprinkle with salt and pepper. Grill pork, covered with grill lid, 15 to 18 minutes or until a meat thermometer inserted into thickest portion registers 145°, turning twice and basting with ¼ cup barbecue sauce. Remove from grill; let stand 5 minutes before slicing.

3. Cut tenderloins into ½-inch-thick slices, and serve on rolls with remaining barbecue sauce and spicy pickles.

GRILLED PORK TENDERLOIN SANDWICHES

Makes: 6 servings   Hands-On Time: 34 min.   Total Time: 45 min.

1   tsp. garlic powder
1   tsp. salt
1   tsp. dry mustard
½   tsp. coarsely ground pepper

2   (¾-lb.) pork tenderloins
Vegetable cooking spray
6   whole wheat hamburger buns
6   Tbsp. Vidalia Onion BBQ Sauce

1. Stir together first 4 ingredients; rub pork tenderloins evenly with seasoning mixture. Lightly coat pork with cooking spray.

2. Preheat grill to 350° to 400° (medium-high) heat. Grill pork, covered with grill lid, 10 to 12 minutes on each side or until a meat thermometer inserted into thickest portions registers 145°.

Remove from grill, and let stand 10 minutes. Chop or slice, and serve on hamburger buns. Drizzle each sandwich with Vidalia Onion BBQ Sauce.

VIDALIA ONION BBQ SAUCE

Makes: about 2½ cups
Hands-On Time: 10 min.
Total Time: 30 min.

1   medium-size Vidalia or sweet onion, finely chopped
1   cup ketchup
2   Tbsp. brown sugar
2   Tbsp. fresh lemon juice
2   Tbsp. cider vinegar
2   Tbsp. Worcestershire sauce
1   Tbsp. olive oil
1   garlic clove, minced
½   tsp. salt
½   tsp. pepper

1. Whisk together all ingredients and ½ cup water in a large saucepan; bring to a boil over medium heat. Reduce heat to low, and simmer, stirring occasionally, 20 minutes.

EAST CAROLINA COUNTRY-STYLE RIBS

Makes: 6 servings   **Hands-On Time: 43 min.**   **Total Time: 1 hour, 13 min.**

Searing the ribs over high heat first locks in the moisture of the meat and then cooking over low heat makes them moist.

4   lb. bone-in country-style pork ribs
⅓   cup Pork Dry Rub (page 28)

2   cups Eastern Carolina Vinegar Sauce (page 24), divided

1. Sprinkle ribs with Pork Dry Rub; let stand 10 minutes. Fill a spray bottle with ½ cup East Carolina Vinegar Sauce.

2. Preheat grill to 400° to 450° (high) heat. Grill ribs, covered with grill lid, 5 minutes on each side to sear. Reduce grill temperature to 250° to 300° (low) heat.

3. Grill, covered with grill lid, 15 minutes on each side, spraying occasionally with vinegar sauce. Turn off 1 side of grill. Arrange ribs over unlit side, and grill, covered with grill lid, 30 minutes or until a meat thermometer inserted into thickest portion registers 145°, spraying with vinegar sauce occasionally. Let stand 10 minutes before serving. Serve with remaining 1½ cups vinegar sauce.

TROY'S TIP

Country-style ribs are not ribs at all. They're more of a pork chop.

PEACH-GLAZED PORK CHOPS

Makes: 4 servings   Hands-On Time: 31 min.   Total Time: 36 min.

If you have any peach preserves mixture left over after basting the peaches, serve it with the chops. However, any remaining preserves mixture used for basting the pork should be discarded.

1 (18-oz.) jar peach preserves	4 (8-oz.) bone-in pork loin chops (1½ inches thick)
¼ cup soy sauce	¼ tsp. salt
2 Tbsp. grated fresh ginger	¼ tsp. freshly ground pepper
2 tsp. olive oil	4 large peaches, halved

1. Preheat grill to 350° to 400° (medium-high) heat. Bring preserves, soy sauce, and ginger to a boil in a small saucepan. Remove from heat; reserve ½ cup to baste peaches.

2. Rub oil over pork chops; sprinkle with salt and pepper. Grill pork chops, covered with grill lid, 5 to 7 minutes on each side or until a meat thermometer inserted into thickest portion registers 145°, basting often with 1 cup peach preserves mixture.

3. At the same time, grill peaches, covered with grill lid, 2 to 3 minutes on each side or until tender, basting often with reserved ½ cup peach preserves mixture. Let pork chops stand 5 minutes before serving.

BROWN SUGAR PORK CHOPS WITH PEACH BBQ SAUCE

Makes: 4 servings   Hands-On Time: 45 min.   Total Time: 1 hour, 20 min.

The brown sugar marinade caramelizes beautifully on the pork chops when you grill them, and the peach BBQ sauce with fragrant fresh ginger is a perfect match.

¾ cup firmly packed dark brown sugar
¼ cup kosher salt
2 cups boiling water
3 cups ice cubes
4 bone-in pork loin chops (about 2 lb.)
1 medium-size sweet onion, finely chopped
1 Tbsp. canola oil
1 garlic clove, minced

1 (1-inch) piece fresh ginger, peeled and grated
1½ cups ketchup
½ cup peach preserves or jam
2 large peaches (about 1 lb.), peeled and cut into ¾-inch chunks
2 Tbsp. cider vinegar
Kosher salt and freshly ground pepper to taste
Garnish: fresh oregano sprigs

1. Combine sugar and salt in a large bowl; add boiling water, stirring until sugar and salt dissolve. Stir in ice cubes to cool mixture. Add pork chops; cover and chill 30 minutes.

2. Meanwhile, sauté onion in hot oil in a medium saucepan over medium heat 2 minutes or until tender. Add garlic and ginger; cook, stirring constantly, 45 to 60 seconds or until fragrant. Add ketchup, peach preserves, and peaches. Reduce heat to low, and simmer, stirring occasionally, 30 minutes or until sauce thickens. Add vinegar; season with kosher salt and freshly ground pepper to taste. Remove from heat.

3. Remove pork from brine, discarding brine. Rinse pork well, and pat dry with paper towels.

4. Preheat grill to 350° to 400° (medium-high) heat. Pour half of peach mixture into a bowl; reserve remaining mixture. Season both sides of pork with desired amount of kosher salt and freshly ground pepper.

5. Grill pork, covered with grill lid, 5 to 6 minutes on each side or until a meat thermometer inserted into thickest portion of each chop registers 145°, basting pork occasionally with peach mixture in bowl. Remove pork from grill; let stand 5 minutes before serving. Serve with reserved peach mixture. Garnish, if desired.

TROY'S TIP

Adding ice cubes to the hot sugar and salt mixture not only cools everything down, it also creates a quick brine in which to soak the pork chops. In just a short 30 minutes, the brine will penetrate the meat to lock in moisture and a ton of flavor.

MOLASSES-GLAZED PORK STEAKS

Makes: 4 servings   **Hands-On Time: 30 min.**   **Total Time: 8 hours, 30 min.**

Pork steaks are cut from the Boston butt or whole pork shoulder.

1	(12-oz.) jar molasses (1½ cups)	1	Tbsp. grated fresh ginger
½	cup cider vinegar	3	garlic cloves, minced
½	cup soy sauce	4	bone-in pork steaks (about 4 lb.)

1. Whisk together first 5 ingredients. Pour marinade into a large zip-top plastic freezer bag; add pork steaks, turning to coat. Seal and chill 8 hours.

2. Preheat grill to 300° to 350° (medium) heat. Remove steaks from marinade, reserving 1 cup marinade. Bring reserved marinade to a boil in a saucepan over medium-high heat, and boil 3 minutes. Remove from heat, and let cool slightly.

3. Grill steaks, covered with grill lid, 6 to 8 minutes on each side or until a meat thermometer inserted into thickest portion registers 145°, basting twice with reserved marinade. Remove from grill, and let stand 5 minutes before serving.

PLUM-GLAZED SAUSAGE

Makes: 8 to 10 servings   **Hands-On Time: 20 min.**   **Total Time: 25 min.**

Offer Bratwurst, Bockwurst, and weisswurst with fresh chicken or spicy pork sausage.

¾	cup plum preserves	¼	tsp. freshly ground pepper
2	Tbsp. balsamic vinegar	2	lb. assorted fresh sausages
2	tsp. chopped fresh thyme		

1. Preheat grill to 300° to 350° (medium) heat. Cook first 4 ingredients in a small saucepan over low heat, stirring often, 5 minutes; reserve half of mixture.

2. Grill sausages, covered with grill lid, 10 to 12 minutes or until done, turning occasionally and brushing with remaining half of plum mixture during last 5 minutes of grilling. Remove from heat; let stand 5 minutes. Serve with reserved plum mixture.

Plum-Glazed Sausage

GRILLED ANDOUILLE SAUSAGE WITH PICKLES

Makes: 8 appetizer servings   Hands-On Time: 12 min.   Total Time: 12 min.

2   lb. andouille sausage   Uncle Hoyt's Bread-and-Butter Pickles

1. Preheat grill to 350° to 400° (medium-high) heat. Grill sausage 5 minutes or until done, turning occasionally. Cut sausage diagonally into ¼-inch-thick slices, and serve with Uncle Hoyt's Bread-and-Butter Pickles.

UNCLE HOYT'S BREAD-AND-BUTTER PICKLES

Makes: 14 (1-pt.) jars   Hands-On Time: 2 hours, 10 min.   Total Time: 5 hours, 20 min.

This recipe is from James T. Farmer, III, author of *A Time to Plant*.

25 to 30 medium cucumbers (about 9½ lb.)   4   cups sugar
8   large onions   2   Tbsp. mustard seeds
2   large bell peppers   1   tsp. ground turmeric
½   cup pickling salt   ½   tsp. whole cloves
5   cups white vinegar

1. Cut cucumbers into ¼-inch-thick slices and onions into ⅛-inch-thick slices. Chop bell peppers. Place vegetables in a bowl; toss with pickling salt. Let stand 3 hours; drain.

2. Bring vinegar, sugar, mustard seeds, turmeric, and cloves to a boil in a large stockpot, boiling just until sugar dissolves. Add drained cucumber mixture, and cook, stirring often, 7 to 10 minutes or until mixture is thoroughly heated and cucumber peels turn dark green. Pack half of hot mixture in 7 (1-pt.) hot, sterilized jars, filling to ½ inch from top. Remove air bubbles by gently stirring with a long wooden skewer. Cover at once with metal lids, and screw on bands. Process in boiling water bath 10 minutes. Repeat procedure with remaining mixture and 7 more hot, sterilized jars.

TROY'S TIP

SWEET NO-COOK PICKLES

No time to can your own pickles? Try these instead. As the name says, these pickles don't need to be cooked. Store in the refrigerator up to 2 weeks.

Drain 1 (46-oz.) jar dill pickles; cut pickles into ¼-inch-thick slices. Return to pickle jar. Gradually add 2 cups sugar, tapping bottom of jar gently on a flat surface to allow sugar to settle in jar. Add 1 Tbsp. white wine vinegar. Cover with lid, and let stand at room temperature 1 hour, shaking jar occasionally. Chill 8 hours, shaking jar occasionally. Store in refrigerator up to 2 weeks.

SWEET-HEAT HOT DOGS

Makes: 8 servings   Hands-On Time: 30 min.   Total Time: 30 min.

Take hot dog toppings beyond traditional sauerkraut and mustard by dressing with sweet-hot pickles, shredded red cabbage, and a creamy topping made of mayo, whole grain mustard, and hot chili sauce.

¾ cup mayonnaise
1   Tbsp. whole grain mustard
1   green onion, minced
2   Tbsp. Asian Sriracha hot chili sauce, divided

8   hot dogs
8   hot dog buns, toasted
1   cup chopped sweet-hot pickles
2   cups shredded red cabbage

1. Preheat grill to 350° to 400° (medium-high) heat.

2. Combine first 3 ingredients and 1 Tbsp. chili sauce in a small bowl. Brush hot dogs with remaining 1 Tbsp. chili sauce.

3. Grill hot dogs, covered with grill lid, 4 to 6 minutes or until thoroughly heated. Place hot dogs in buns, and top with mayonnaise mixture. Sprinkle with chopped pickles and shredded cabbage.

⇌ HOW TO SHRED CABBAGE ⇌

GRILLED PEPPERS AND SAUSAGE WITH CHEESE GRITS

Makes: 6 servings   **Hands-On Time: 37 min.**   **Total Time: 37 min.**

Grill sausage alongside bell peppers and onions, and serve over quick-cooking Parmesan grits for a hearty one-dish meal.

2   medium-size red bell peppers, cut into quarters
2   medium-size sweet onions, cut into quarters
2   Tbsp. olive oil
1   tsp. fresh thyme leaves
1   tsp. salt, divided
1   (19.76-oz.) package garlic pork sausage links

2   (14-oz.) cans chicken broth
1   cup uncooked quick-cooking grits
2   Tbsp. butter
1   cup grated Parmesan cheese
⅓   cup chopped fresh basil
½   tsp. freshly ground black pepper
Garnish: basil leaves

1. Preheat grill to 350° to 400° (medium-high) heat. Toss peppers and onions with olive oil, thyme, and ½ tsp. salt. Grill pepper mixture and sausage at the same time, covered with grill lid. Grill pepper mixture, turning occasionally, 8 to 10 minutes or until wilted. Grill sausage 5 minutes on each side or until done.

2. Bring remaining ½ tsp. salt, chicken broth, and ½ cup water to a boil in a 3-qt. saucepan; slowly stir in grits, reduce heat, and simmer 12 minutes or until thickened and creamy, stirring often. Remove from heat, and stir in butter and next 3 ingredients.

3. Coarsely chop peppers and onions, and slice sausage into 1-inch pieces. Serve sausage-and-pepper mixture over hot cooked grits. Garnish, if desired.

PECAN-CRUSTED PORK BURGERS WITH DRIED APRICOT-CHIPOTLE MAYONNAISE

Makes: 4 servings   Hands-On Time: 27 min.   Total Time: 27 min.

Ground pork is becoming more available in the meat case. You can also ask your butcher to grind it. Usually the lean-to-fat ratio is similar to ground chuck.

Vegetable cooking spray
1½ lb. lean ground pork
2   Tbsp. reserved mayonnaise mixture from Dried Apricot-Chipotle Mayonnaise
1   Tbsp. butter, melted
½   cup finely chopped pecans

½   tsp. salt
¼   tsp. pepper
4   French hamburger buns, split
4   Bibb lettuce leaves
Dried Apricot-Chipotle Mayonnaise

1. Coat cold cooking grate of grill with cooking spray, and place on grill. Preheat grill to 350° to 400° (medium-high) heat.

2. Gently combine pork and reserved 2 Tbsp. mayonnaise mixture until blended, using hands. Shape into 4 (4-inch-wide, 1-inch-thick) patties.

3. Whisk together butter and next 3 ingredients in a small bowl until well blended. Sprinkle each patty with about 2 Tbsp. pecan mixture (about 1 Tbsp. on each side), gently pressing to adhere.

4. Grill pecan-covered pork patties, covered with grill lid, 6 to 8 minutes on each side or until a meat thermometer inserted into centers registers 145°.

5. Grill buns, cut sides down, 1 to 2 minutes or until lightly toasted. Serve burgers on buns with lettuce and Dried Apricot-Chipotle Mayonnaise.

DRIED APRICOT-CHIPOTLE MAYONNAISE

Makes: about 1 cup   Hands-On Time: 10 min.   Total Time: 25 min.

Don't shortcut the soak time for the apricots. The tart lime juice balances the concentrated sweetness of this dried fruit.

½   cup dried apricots
¼   cup hot water
2   Tbsp. fresh lime juice
½   cup mayonnaise

1   canned chipotle chile pepper in adobo sauce, chopped
2   Tbsp. finely chopped green onion
1   Tbsp. adobo sauce from can

1. Combine dried apricots, hot water, and lime juice in a bowl. Let stand 15 minutes; drain. Pat apricots dry, and coarsely chop.

2. Combine mayonnaise and next 3 ingredients; reserve 2 Tbsp. mixture for Pecan-Crusted Pork Burgers. Stir apricots into remaining mayonnaise mixture. Cover and chill until ready to serve.

Put Some South in Your Mouth

HOT
CHIX

MARINATED CHICKEN QUARTERS

Makes: 4 servings   Hands-On Time: 1 hour   Total Time: 9 hours

Bone-in chicken breasts can be used in place of the chicken quarters.

½ **cup butter, melted**
½ **cup fresh lemon juice**
1 **Tbsp. paprika**
1 **Tbsp. dried oregano**
1 **tsp. garlic salt**

1 **Tbsp. chopped fresh cilantro**
1 **tsp. ground cumin**
1 **(2½-lb.) whole chicken, quartered**
½ **tsp. salt**
½ **tsp. pepper**

1. Whisk together first 7 ingredients; reserve ½ cup butter mixture for basting, and chill.

2. Sprinkle chicken evenly with salt and pepper. Place in a shallow dish or zip-top plastic freezer bag; pour remaining butter mixture over chicken. Cover or seal, and chill 8 hours.

3. Preheat grill to 350° to 400° (medium-high) heat. Remove chicken from marinade; discard marinade. Grill, covered with grill lid, 40 to 45 minutes or until done, basting often with reserved butter mixture and turning once.

TROY'S TIP

Oftentimes, the meat counter will sell "Pick of the Chick" chicken pieces already cut up for you. They're great for fried chicken recipes but also work here, too.

SOUTH-OF-THE-BORDER BBQ CHICKEN

Makes: 4 servings   Hands-On Time: 47 min.   Total Time: 47 min., plus 1 day for marinating

Serve this Southwestern-flavored chicken over a bed of Mexican rice, or slice it for soft tacos.

1½ cups fresh lime juice
1   cup olive oil
½   cup chopped fresh cilantro
2   tsp. seasoned salt

2   tsp. freshly ground pepper
½   tsp. ancho chile powder
8   garlic cloves, minced
4   skinned and boned chicken breasts (about 2 lb.)

1. Whisk together first 7 ingredients in a small bowl; reserve 1 cup for basting, and chill. Place remaining marinade in a large shallow dish or zip-top plastic freezer bag; add chicken, turning to coat. Cover or seal, and chill 24 hours, turning once.

2. Preheat grill to 300° to 350° (medium) heat. Remove chicken from marinade, discarding marinade. Grill chicken, covered with grill lid, 12 to 13 minutes on each side or until done, basting frequently with reserved 1 cup marinade.

TROY'S TIP

This recipe uses ancho chile powder, a spice made from ground dried poblano chiles. It's less spicy than most peppers and offers a sweet, rich pepper flavor without overpowering heat.

SWEET MUSTARD-GLAZED CHICKEN BREASTS

Makes: 4 servings   Hands-On Time: 19 min.   Total Time: 49 min.

Chicken breasts are a natural with this marinade, but the maple-mustard flavor also works well with turkey, pork, and salmon.

½ **cup Dijon mustard**
¼ **cup maple syrup**
2 **Tbsp. white vinegar**
2 **Tbsp. lite soy sauce**

½ **tsp. coarsely ground pepper**
⅛ **tsp. salt**
4 **skinned and boned chicken breasts (about 2 lb.)**

1. Preheat grill to 350° to 400° (medium-high) heat. Whisk together first 6 ingredients in a small bowl. Reserve ½ cup mustard mixture to serve with cooked chicken.

2. Pour remaining ½ cup mustard mixture in a large shallow dish or zip-top plastic freezer bag; add chicken, turning to coat. Cover or seal, and chill 30 minutes. Remove chicken from marinade, discarding marinade.

3. Grill chicken, covered with grill lid, 7 to 8 minutes on each side or until done. Serve with reserved ½ cup mustard mixture.

YOU
MIGHT GIVE
SOME SERIOUS
THOUGHT TO
THANKING YOUR
LUCKY STARS
YOU'RE IN
TEXAS!

SMOTHERED GRILLED CHICKEN BREASTS

Makes: 4 servings   Hands-On Time: 21 min.   Total Time: 21 min.

Stay out of the kitchen, and throw the whole dinner on the grill. There's not a thing missing from this meal unless you want to toss in some grilled garlic bread on the side.

4   skinned and boned chicken breasts
    (about 2 lb.)
¾   tsp. kosher salt, divided
⅜   tsp. pepper, divided
⅔   cup bottled sweet red barbecue sauce,
    divided

4   (0.4-oz.) provolone cheese slices
1   large red bell pepper
1   sweet onion, cut in half crosswise
2   portobello mushroom caps, stemmed and
    gills removed
1   small garlic clove, minced

1. Preheat grill to 350° to 400° (medium-high) heat. Sprinkle chicken with ¼ tsp. salt and ⅛ tsp. pepper. Grill chicken, covered with grill lid, 5 to 6 minutes on each side or until chicken is done, basting occasionally with ⅓ cup barbecue sauce. Top with cheese; grill 1 minute or until cheese is melted. Grill bell pepper, onion, and mushroom caps, covered with grill lid, 5 to 6 minutes or until vegetables are tender and bell pepper is slightly charred, turning occasionally.

2. Let chicken stand 5 minutes. Cut bell pepper in half lengthwise; remove and discard seeds and membranes. Cut bell pepper into strips. Slice onion and mushroom caps.

3. Toss together grilled vegetables, remaining ½ tsp. salt, remaining ¼ tsp. pepper, remaining ⅓ cup barbecue sauce, and garlic in a medium bowl. Serve vegetables with chicken.

PIT STOP

Puckett's Grocery
Franklin, TN

This local favorite has great barbecue and live music—a match made in heaven! The original location was founded by the Puckett family in the 1950s in the Leiper's Fork area, and it served as a local country store for groceries, gas, and food. When it was sold to Andy Marshall, a local of nearby Franklin, Tennessee, he realized what he had "was a restaurant pretending to be a grocery store." Marshall uses the barbecuing techniques he learned while growing up in Memphis to create slow-smoked ribs, chicken, and pork as well as other Southern favorites like chicken and waffles and meat-and-three lunches. They even serve breakfast!

CURRIED CHICKEN KABOBS

Makes: 4 servings   Hands-On Time: 23 min.   Total Time: 23 min., plus 1 day for marinating

Be sure to heavily coat the food grate of your grill with cooking spray to prevent the yogurt-based marinade from sticking.

4   skinned and boned chicken breasts, cut into 1½-inch pieces
1   Tbsp. Moroccan seasoning blend
1   tsp. kosher salt, divided
¼   tsp. freshly ground black pepper
¾   cup fat-free yogurt
1   Tbsp. curry powder
2   Tbsp. fresh lime juice

1   Tbsp. grated fresh ginger
2   tsp. sugar
¼   tsp. ground red pepper
3   garlic cloves, minced
Vegetable cooking spray
4   (12-inch) metal skewers
4   lime wedges

1. Toss chicken with Moroccan seasoning blend, ½ tsp. salt, and black pepper in a medium bowl. Stir together remaining ½ tsp. salt, yogurt, and next 6 ingredients in a small bowl. Pour ½ cup yogurt mixture into a large shallow dish or zip-top plastic freezer bag; add seasoned chicken, turning to coat.

Cover or seal, and chill 24 hours. Cover and chill remaining ½ cup yogurt mixture to serve with cooked chicken.

2. Coat cold cooking grate of grill with cooking spray, and place on grill. Preheat grill to 350° to 400° (medium-high) heat.

3. Remove chicken from marinade, discarding marinade. Thread chicken onto skewers, leaving ¼ inch between pieces. Grill kabobs, covered with grill lid, 6 minutes on each side or until chicken is done. Serve kabobs with reserved yogurt mixture and lime wedges.

SMOKY CHICKEN BBQ KABOBS

Makes: 8 servings   Hands-On Time: 20 min.   Total Time: 20 min.

Rub the chicken cubes in a smoky-flavored mixture of brown sugar, ground chipotle chile pepper, and cumin, and grill on skewers with cherry tomatoes and onion wedges. Serve with a tangy mayonnaise-based barbecue sauce.

4   skinned and boned chicken breasts
    (about 2 lb.)
½   large red onion, cut into fourths and
    separated into pieces

1   pt. cherry tomatoes
8   (8-inch) metal skewers
Smoky-Sweet BBQ Rub (page 29)
White BBQ Sauce (page 23)

1. Preheat grill to 350° to 400° (medium-high) heat. Cut chicken into 1-inch cubes. Thread chicken, onion, and tomatoes alternately onto skewers, leaving ¼ inch between pieces. Sprinkle kabobs with Smoky-Sweet BBQ Rub.

2. Grill kabobs, covered with grill lid, 4 to 5 minutes on each side. Serve with White BBQ Sauce.

Smoky Steak BBQ Kabobs:
Substitute 2 lb. top sirloin steak, trimmed, for chicken. Proceed with recipe as directed.

JERK CHICKEN KABOBS

Makes: 8 servings   Hands-On Time: 44 min.
Total Time: 8 hours, 58 min., plus 1 day for marinating

A refreshingly cool cucumber sauce tames the kick of habanero heat, traditional in jerk marinade. Be sure to wear gloves when halving and seeding the habanero pepper and when threading the chicken on the skewers to prevent the pepper from burning your skin.

4 garlic cloves, halved	2 Tbsp. soy sauce
½ habanero pepper, seeded	2 tsp. ground allspice
1 cup coarsely chopped green onions	2 tsp. pepper
⅓ cup chopped red onion	½ tsp. ground cinnamon
¼ cup fresh lime juice	½ tsp. freshly grated nutmeg
2 Tbsp. salt	3¼ lb. skinned and boned chicken breasts, cut
2 Tbsp. light brown sugar	into 1-inch pieces
1 Tbsp. fresh thyme leaves	8 (12-inch) metal skewers
3 Tbsp. olive oil	Cool Cucumber Sauce (page 172)

1. With food processor running, drop garlic and habanero pepper through food chute; process until minced. Add green onions and next 11 ingredients; process 30 seconds or until smooth, scraping sides of processor bowl once. Pour onion mixture into a large shallow dish or zip-top plastic freezer bag; add chicken, turning to coat. Cover or seal, and chill 24 hours.

2. Preheat grill to 350° to 400° (medium-high) heat. Remove chicken from marinade, discarding marinade. Thread chicken onto skewers, leaving ¼ inch between pieces.

3. Grill kabobs, covered with grill lid, 14 minutes, turning after 7 minutes. Serve with Cool Cucumber Sauce.

COOL CUCUMBER SAUCE

Makes: about 1 cup Hands-On Time: 8 min. Total Time: 8 min.

You can use this creamy concoction as a dipping sauce for grilled vegetables or a sauce for spicy grilled meats.

1½ cups peeled, seeded, and chopped
    cucumber
½ cup mayonnaise
⅓ cup sour cream
1 Tbsp. cider vinegar

1½ tsp. Dijon mustard
1½ tsp. chopped garlic
¼ tsp. kosher salt
Dash of ground red pepper

1. Process all ingredients in a food processor 30 seconds or until smooth. Cover and chill until ready to serve.

❧ HOW TO PEEL, SEED & CHOP CUCUMBER ❧

CHICKEN-AND-BACON SATAY

Makes: 16 to 20 kabobs   Hands-On Time: 50 min.   Total Time: 1 hour, 35 min.

Satay is an Indonesian version of kabobs: thinly sliced marinated meat grilled on a skewer and served with peanut sauce.

4 skinned and boned chicken thighs (about 1 lb.)	½ tsp. dried crushed red pepper
½ cup lite soy sauce	16 to 20 (4-inch) wooden skewers
⅓ cup sake	8 to 10 fully-cooked bacon slices, cut in half crosswise
2 Tbsp. light brown sugar	Peanut Sauce
1 Tbsp. grated fresh ginger	Garnish: thinly sliced green onions

1. Place chicken between 2 sheets of plastic wrap, and flatten to ¼-inch thickness using a rolling pin or flat side of a meat mallet. Cut chicken into 16 to 20 (1-inch) strips.

2. Combine soy sauce and next 4 ingredients in a large zip-top plastic freezer bag; add chicken, turning to coat. Seal and chill 45 minutes, turning once.

3. Meanwhile, soak skewers in water 30 minutes; drain.

4. Preheat grill to 350° to 400° (medium-high) heat. Remove chicken from marinade; discard marinade. Thread 1 bacon and 1 chicken strip onto each skewer.

5. Grill skewers, covered with grill lid, 4 to 5 minutes on each side or until chicken is done. Serve skewers with Peanut Sauce. Garnish, if desired.

PEANUT SAUCE

Makes: about 1⅓ cups   Hands-On Time: 10 min.   Total Time: 10 min.

½ cup creamy peanut butter	3 Tbsp. fresh lime juice
⅓ cup lite soy sauce	3 Tbsp. honey
¼ cup loosely packed fresh cilantro leaves	3 Tbsp. dark sesame oil

1. Process all ingredients in a blender or food processor until smooth. Add 1 to 2 Tbsp. water, 1 tsp. at a time, processing until desired consistency is reached.

SWEET-HEAT BONELESS CHICKEN THIGHS

Makes: 10 servings   Hands-On Time: 5 min.   Total Time: 21 min.

Orange marmalade and horseradish combine to give these grilled thighs a sweet-heat flavor profile.

3   lb. skinned and boned chicken thighs
½   tsp. salt
½   tsp. pepper
½   cup orange marmalade

¼   cup chopped green onions
2   Tbsp. soy sauce
1   Tbsp. refrigerated horseradish

1. Preheat grill to 300° to 350° (medium) heat. Sprinkle chicken with salt and pepper. Stir together marmalade, green onions, soy sauce, and horseradish in a small bowl.

2. Grill chicken, covered with grill lid, 8 minutes on each side or until a meat thermometer inserted into thickest portion registers 180°, basting frequently with marmalade mixture.

TROY'S TIP

Boneless skinless chicken thighs offer the convenience of a quick cook time. You can buy them already skinned and boned. Or, if you prefer, substitute bone-in chicken thighs and remove the skin to prevent greasiness. You'll need to increase the cook time to 12 to 13 minutes per side.

SWEET GINGER CHICKEN THIGHS

Makes: 12 servings   Hands-On Time: 28 min.   Total Time: 8 hours, 38 min.

This recipe is good using skin-on or skinless chicken thighs. Either way, you'll want to monitor the grill at medium heat and watch for flare-ups.

2   (6-oz.) cans pineapple juice
3   Tbsp. grated fresh ginger
3   Tbsp. soy sauce
2   Tbsp. sesame oil
2   Tbsp. light brown sugar

1   tsp. kosher salt
¾   tsp. coarsely ground pepper
3   green onions, thinly sliced
4   lb. skin-on, bone-in chicken thighs

1. Whisk together first 8 ingredients; reserve 1 cup for sauce. Pour remaining marinade into a large zip-top plastic freezer bag; add chicken. Seal and chill 8 hours.

2. Pour reserved 1 cup marinade into a small saucepan. Bring to a boil over medium-high heat; reduce heat, and simmer 10 minutes or until marinade is slightly thickened and reduced to ½ cup.

3. Preheat grill to 300° to 350° (medium) heat. Remove chicken from marinade; discard marinade. Grill chicken, covered with grill lid, 8 to 10 minutes on each side or until a meat thermometer registers 180°. Brush chicken with reserved marinade.

HOW TO PEEL & GRATE GINGER

SPICY HONEY-LIME GRILLED DRUMSTICKS

Makes: 4 servings Hands-On Time: 40 min. Total Time: 1 hour, 10 min.

8 chicken drumsticks
1 tsp. salt
½ tsp. pepper

Vegetable cooking spray
Spicy Honey-Lime BBQ Sauce
Garnish: lime wedges

1. Sprinkle chicken with salt and pepper. Let stand, covered, 30 minutes. Coat cold cooking grate of grill with cooking spray, and place on grill. Preheat grill to 350° to 400° (medium-high) heat.

2. Grill chicken, covered with grill lid, 5 to 10 minutes on each side or until browned. Reduce grill temperature to 250° to 300° (low) heat; grill chicken, covered with grill lid, 20 to 30 minutes.

3. Prepare Spicy Honey-Lime BBQ Sauce. Reserve 1 cup sauce. Brush chicken with remaining barbecue sauce. Grill, covered with grill lid, 10 more minutes or until done. Serve chicken with reserved 1 cup barbecue sauce. Garnish, if desired.

SPICY HONEY-LIME BBQ SAUCE

Makes: about 2 cups Hands-On Time: 20 min. Total Time: 20 min.

¼ cup butter
1 medium onion, diced (about 1 cup)
1 (12-oz.) bottle chili sauce

¼ cup honey
2 Tbsp. fresh lime juice
¼ tsp. pepper

1. Melt butter in a small saucepan over medium heat; add onion, and sauté 4 to 5 minutes or until tender. Stir in chili sauce, next 3 ingredients, and ⅓ cup water; bring to a boil. Reduce heat to low, and simmer 5 minutes. Store in refrigerator up to 1 week.

LEMON-GARLIC DRUMSTICKS

Makes: 4 to 5 servings   Hands-On Time: 32 min.   Total Time: 8 hours, 32 min.

We recommend marinating the chicken at least 8 hours and up to 24 hours. The longer the chicken marinates, the more flavorful it will be. Look for the marinade for chicken with white wine and herbs next to the Worcestershire sauce in your supermarket.

6   Tbsp. fresh lemon juice
¼   cup marinade for chicken with white wine and herbs
3   Tbsp. olive oil
1   tsp. kosher salt
1   tsp. freshly ground pepper
8   garlic cloves, chopped
3   lb. chicken drumsticks

1. Combine lemon juice and next 5 ingredients in a large shallow dish or zip-top plastic freezer bag; add chicken, turning to coat. Cover or seal, and chill 8 to 24 hours, turning once.

2. Preheat grill to 300° to 350° (medium) heat. Remove chicken from marinade; discard marinade. Grill chicken, covered with grill lid, 24 minutes or until done, turning often.

SPICY GRILLED WINGS

Makes: 12 servings   Hands-On Time: 1 hour   Total Time: 1 hour

2   tsp. ground chipotle chile pepper
2   tsp. black pepper
2   tsp. salt, divided
4½ to 5 lb. chicken wings
1   Tbsp. olive oil
3   Tbsp. butter
½   cup chopped onion
2   garlic cloves, pressed
1   cup cider vinegar
1   (8-oz.) can tomato sauce
1   (6-oz.) can tomato paste
2   Tbsp. light brown sugar
2   Tbsp. Worcestershire sauce
2   tsp. hot sauce
Blue Cheese Sauce

1. Light 1 side of grill, heating to 350° to 400° (medium-high) heat. Combine first 2 ingredients and 1 tsp. salt. Cut off chicken wing tips, and discard; cut wings in half at joint. Toss wings with oil. Sprinkle chicken with pepper mixture, and toss.

2. Arrange wings over unlit side of grill, and grill, covered with grill lid, 18 to 20 minutes on each side or until done.

3. Meanwhile, melt butter in a saucepan over medium-high heat; add onion and garlic, and sauté 5 minutes or until tender. Reduce heat to medium. Add vinegar, next 5 ingredients, and remaining 1 tsp. salt. Cook, stirring occasionally, 10 to 12 minutes or until bubbly.

4. Transfer wings to a clean bowl; add half of butter mixture, reserving remaining mixture. Toss wings gently to coat. Place wings on lit side of grill. Grill, covered with grill lid, 10 minutes or until browned, turning occasionally. Toss wings with reserved butter mixture. Serve with Blue Cheese Sauce.

BLUE CHEESE SAUCE

Makes: about 2 cups   Hands-On Time: 10 min.   Total Time: 10 min.

1   (8-oz.) container sour cream
⅓   cup buttermilk
1   (4-oz.) wedge blue cheese, crumbled
2   Tbsp. chopped fresh chives
1   tsp. lemon zest

1   Tbsp. fresh lemon juice
1   tsp. coarse-grained mustard
½   tsp. salt
¼   tsp. pepper

1. Stir together all ingredients. Cover and chill until ready to serve.

GRILLED TURKEY BREAST

Makes: 8 servings   Hands-On Time: 1 hour, 25 min.   Total Time: 9 hours, 35 min.

⅓ cup kosher salt
⅓ cup sugar
3 bay leaves
2 jalapeño peppers, halved
2 Tbsp. cumin seeds
Large, deep, food-safe container
1 (5- to 6-lb.) boned, skin-on fresh
   turkey breast*

Vegetable cooking spray
1 Tbsp. table salt
1 Tbsp. cumin seeds
1 Tbsp. paprika
2 tsp. freshly ground black pepper
1 tsp. ground coriander
1 tsp. dried oregano
Parsley-Mint Salsa Verde

1. Stir together kosher salt, next 4 ingredients, and 2 qt. water in a large, deep, food-safe container or stockpot until sugar is dissolved. Add turkey. Chill 8 hours or overnight, turning once.

2. Coat cold cooking grate of grill with cooking spray, and place on grill. Light 1 side of grill, heating to 350° to 400° (medium-high) heat; leaveother side unlit. Remove turkey from brine. Rinse turkey, drain well, and pat dry with paper towels.

3. Stir together table salt and next 5 ingredients. Rub skin of turkey with mixture.

4. Place turkey, skin side down, over lit side of grill, and grill, without grill lid, 4 to 5 minutes or until slightly charred. Transfer to unlit side, skin side up. Grill, covered with grill lid, 30 to 40 minutes or until a meat thermometer inserted into thickest portion registers 165°. Return turkey, skin side down, to lit side, and grill, covered with grill lid, 4 to 5 minutes or until skin is crisp.

5. Remove turkey from heat; cover loosely with aluminum foil. Let stand 10 minutes. Serve with Parsley-Mint Salsa Verde.

*FROZEN TURKEY BREAST, thawed, may be substituted.

PARSLEY-MINT SALSA VERDE

Makes: 1¾ cups   Hands-On Time: 15 min.   Total Time: 35 min.

- ⅔ cup extra virgin olive oil
- ⅓ cup sherry vinegar
- ¼ cup finely chopped shallots
- 2 garlic cloves, finely chopped
- 1 tsp. salt
- ½ tsp. freshly ground pepper
- 1 cup chopped fresh flat-leaf parsley
- ¾ cup chopped fresh mint

1. Whisk together first 6 ingredients and 2 Tbsp. water until salt dissolves. Whisk in

ASIAN-GRILLED QUAIL

Makes: 4 servings   Hands-On Time: 45 min.   Total Time: 1 hour, 15 min.

Quail gets a hearty dose of Asian-inspired flavor in this game recipe. Grilling the quail brings out the sweetness of the marinade, infusing the meat with moist, bold flavor.

¼ cup hoisin sauce
2 Tbsp. sesame seeds
3 Tbsp. Asian chili-garlic sauce
3 Tbsp. dark sesame oil
3 Tbsp. honey

1 tsp. ground ginger
8 quail, dressed
1 (14-oz.) can chicken broth
2 tsp. cornstarch
Garnish: sliced green onions or green onion curls

1. Whisk together first 6 ingredients in a shallow dish or large zip-top plastic freezer bag; add quail. Cover or seal, and chill 30 minutes, turning occasionally.

2. Remove quail from marinade, reserving marinade. Light coals on 1 side of grill, heating to 350° to 400° (medium-high) heat; leave other side unlit.

3. Place quail over unlit side, and grill, covered with grill lid, 30 minutes or until done. Pour reserved marinade into a small saucepan. Reserve ¼ cup chicken broth, and add remaining chicken broth to marinade.

4. Bring mixture to a boil over medium-high heat; boil, stirring occasionally, 5 minutes. Whisk together cornstarch and reserved ¼ cup chicken broth until smooth. Whisk into marinade mixture; boil, whisking constantly, 1 minute. Serve with quail; garnish, if desired.

Asian-Grilled Cornish Hens:
Substitute 4 (1- to 1½-lb.) Cornish hens for quail. Grill as directed 45 to 50 minutes or until done.

MUFFULETTA BURGERS

Makes: 6 servings   Hands-On Time: 30 min.   Total Time: 30 min.

Flavors of the famous New Orleans sandwich are transformed into a juicy, piled-high burger everyone will love.

2   lb. lean ground turkey breast
1   tsp. salt
1   tsp. lemon zest
½   cup mayonnaise
¼   cup chopped fresh parsley
½   cup chopped pimiento-stuffed Spanish olives

½   (16-oz.) jar mixed pickled vegetables, drained
2   Tbsp. dried Italian dressing
Hamburger buns
Toppings: salami, ham, and provolone
    cheese slices

1. Preheat grill to 350° to 400° (medium-high) heat. Combine first 5 ingredients gently. Stir olives into meat mixture. Shape mixture into 6 (5-inch) patties.

2. Grill, covered with grill lid, 6 to 7 minutes on each side or until a meat thermometer inserted into thickest portion registers 170°.

3. Pulse pickled vegetables and Italian dressing in a food processor until coarsely chopped. Serve burgers on buns. Top burgers with provolone cheese slices, ham, salami, and vegetable mixture.

FRESH CATCH

GRILLED SEA BASS WITH MANGO SALSA

Makes: 4 servings   Hands-On Time: 14 min.   Total Time: 14 min.

There's no shortage of salsa here, so pile it high on each fish fillet. It's colorful, refreshing, and carries the flavor of this summertime dish.

4   (6-oz.) sea bass fillets
1½ tsp. kosher salt, divided
1½ tsp. freshly ground pepper, divided
2   cups chopped mango

1   cup chopped red bell pepper
⅔   cup chopped green onions
¼   cup chopped fresh cilantro
2   Tbsp. fresh lime juice

1. Preheat grill to 350° to 400° (medium-high) heat. Sprinkle sea bass fillets with 1 tsp. salt and 1 tsp. pepper.

2. Toss together mango, next 4 ingredients, and remaining ½ tsp. salt and ½ tsp. pepper in a medium bowl.

3. Grill fillets, covered with grill lid, 3 minutes on each side or just until fish flakes with a fork. Serve with salsa.

GARLIC-AND-HERB GRILLED HALIBUT

Makes: 4 servings   Hands-On Time: 22 min.   Total Time: 1 hour, 22 min.

Halibut is a very dense, mild-flavored firm white fish. Grouper or haddock are good substitutions.

¼ **cup chopped fresh parsley**

¼ **cup red wine vinegar**

¼ **cup olive oil**

2 **Tbsp. chopped fresh rosemary**

1 **Tbsp. fresh thyme leaves**

1 **tsp. lemon zest**

1½ **Tbsp. fresh lemon juice**

1 **tsp. kosher salt**

1 **tsp. freshly ground pepper**

2 **tsp. anchovy paste**

8 **garlic cloves, pressed**

4 **(6- to 8-oz.) halibut fillets (2 inches thick)**

Vegetable cooking spray

1. Whisk together first 11 ingredients in a small bowl; reserve ¼ cup to serve over cooked fish. Place remaining marinade in a large shallow dish or zip-top plastic freezer bag; add fillets, turning to coat. Cover or seal, and chill 1 hour, turning once.

2. Coat cold cooking grate with cooking spray and place on grill. Preheat grill to 350° to 400° (medium-high) heat.

3. Remove fillets from marinade, discarding marinade. Grill fillets 4 minutes on each side or just until fish flakes with a fork. Remove from grill, and drizzle with reserved ¼ cup marinade before serving.

TROY'S TIP

To easily peel garlic, place the broad side of a chef's knife over the garlic clove. With a swift motion, hit the flat side of the knife with the heel of your hand. The smashing motion will separate the papery skin from the meat of the garlic.

POBLANO FISH TACOS

Makes: 6 servings   **Hands-On Time: 22 min.**   **Total Time: 42 min.**

1   large poblano pepper
1/2   English cucumber, coarsely chopped
1   cup grape tomatoes, quartered
2   Tbsp. chopped red onion
1   garlic clove, minced
1/2   tsp. salt

3   Tbsp. fresh lime juice, divided
4   Tbsp. olive oil, divided
1   Tbsp. mango-lime seafood seasoning
1 1/2   lb. grouper or other firm white fish fillets
12   (6-inch) fajita-size corn tortillas, warmed
Lime wedges

1. Preheat grill to 350° to 400° (medium-high) heat. Grill pepper, covered with grill lid, 3 to 4 minutes or until pepper looks blistered, turning once. Place pepper in a zip-top plastic freezer bag; seal and let stand 10 minutes to loosen skins. Peel pepper; remove and discard seeds. Coarsely chop.

2. Combine pepper, cucumber, next 4 ingredients, 2 Tbsp. lime juice, and 2 Tbsp. olive oil in a bowl.

3. Whisk together seafood seasoning, remaining 1 Tbsp. lime juice, and 2 Tbsp. olive oil in a large shallow dish or zip-top plastic freezer bag; add fish fillets, turning to coat. Cover or seal, and chill 5 minutes, turning once. Remove fish from marinade, discarding marinade.

4. Grill fish, covered with grill lid, 3 to 4 minutes on each side or just until fish begins to flake when poked with the tip of a sharp knife. Cool 5 minutes. Flake fish into bite-size pieces.

5. Serve fish and salsa in warm tortillas with lime wedges.

NOTE: We tested with Weber Mango Lime Seafood Seasoning.

— TRY THIS TWIST —

Top with crumbled queso fresco (fresh Mexican cheese) for a tasty variation.

GRILLED GROUPER WITH CUCUMBER-WATERMELON SALSA

Makes: 4 servings   Hands-On Time: 21 min.   Total Time: 21 min.

- 4 (4-oz.) grouper fillets
- 1 tsp. freshly ground black pepper
- 1 tsp. salt, divided
- 3 Tbsp. olive oil, divided
- 2 cups chopped seedless watermelon
- ¼ cup chopped pitted kalamata olives
- ½ English cucumber, chopped
- 1 small jalapeño pepper, seeded and minced
- 2 Tbsp. minced red onion
- 2 Tbsp. white balsamic vinegar

1. Preheat grill to 350° to 400° (medium-high) heat. Sprinkle grouper with black pepper and ½ tsp. salt. Drizzle with 2 Tbsp. olive oil.

2. Grill fish, covered with grill lid, 3 to 4 minutes on each side or just until fish begins to flake when poked with the tip of a sharp knife.

3. Combine chopped watermelon, next 5 ingredients, and remaining ½ tsp. salt and 1 Tbsp. olive oil. Serve with grilled fish.

HOW TO SEED & MINCE JALAPEÑO PEPPERS

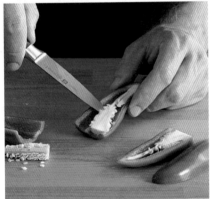

BLACKENED GRILLED CATFISH FILLETS

Makes: 6 servings **Hands-On Time: 12 min.** **Total Time: 12 min.**

Heavily coated with spices, these fillets pair well with grilled corn and a side of slaw.

2 Tbsp. kosher salt
3 Tbsp. paprika
1 tsp. granulated garlic
1 tsp. ground red pepper
1/2 tsp. dried oregano
1/2 tsp. dried thyme

1/2 tsp. freshly ground black pepper
1/2 tsp. ancho chile pepper
6 farm-raised catfish fillets
2 Tbsp. olive oil
Garnish: lemon wedges

1. Preheat grill to 350° to 400° (medium-high) heat. Stir together first 8 ingredients in a small bowl. Rub catfish with oil, and sprinkle with spice mixture. (This should form a paste.)

2. Grill, covered with grill lid, 4 minutes on each side or just until fish flakes with a fork. Garnish with lemon wedges, if desired.

TROY'S TIP

Farm-raised catfish fillets are a great option for a quick-grilled dinner. They're inexpensive and mild, so they soak up the flavor of the rub. You can substitute orange roughy or tilapia fillets, if you'd like.

TROPICAL GRILLED TUNA STEAKS

Makes: 4 servings   Hands-On Time: 12 min.   Total Time: 1 hour, 17 min.

Tuna is best served medium-rare, but if you prefer it more well done, add additional cook time.

1   cup pineapple juice
¼   cup hoisin sauce
2   Tbsp. fresh lime juice
1   Tbsp. chopped fresh cilantro

1   tsp. grated fresh ginger
1   tsp. dark sesame oil
4   (12-oz.) tuna steaks (1 inch thick)

1. Whisk together first 6 ingredients in a small bowl. Place ¾ cup juice mixture in a large shallow dish or zip-top plastic freezer bag; add tuna, turning to coat. Cover or seal, and chill 1 hour, turning once.

2. Preheat grill to 400° to 450° (high) heat. Remove tuna from marinade, discarding marinade.

3. Grill tuna, covered with grill lid, 2 minutes on each side or to desired degree of doneness.

4. Bring remaining ¾ cup juice mixture to a boil in a small saucepan over medium-high heat, and boil 5 minutes or until reduced to ½ cup. Serve with tuna steaks.

GRILLED TUNA SANDWICHES

Makes: 4 sandwiches   **Hands-On Time: 25 min.**   **Total Time: 25 min.**

4   (12-oz.) tuna steaks (1 inch thick)
2   Tbsp. olive oil, divided
½   tsp. salt
½   tsp. black pepper
8   slices sourdough bread
¼   tsp. ground red pepper (optional)

¼   cup finely chopped green onions
¼   cup mayonnaise
2   Tbsp. fresh lime juice
2   tsp. refrigerated horseradish
1   large tomato, thinly sliced
1   ripe avocado, sliced

1. Rub tuna with 1 Tbsp. olive oil, and sprinkle salt and black pepper evenly on both sides of tuna.

2. Preheat grill to 350° to 400° (medium-high) heat. Grill, covered with grill lid, 5 minutes on each side or to desired degree of doneness.

3. Brush bread slices with remaining 1 Tbsp. olive oil, and grill 1 minute on each side or until golden.

4. Flake tuna; combine with ground red pepper, if desired, and next 4 ingredients. Spread tuna mixture evenly on 1 side of 4 bread slices; top with tomato and avocado slices. Cover with remaining 4 bread slices.

TROY'S TIP

One of the great things about the South is that it's warm enough most of the year to grill outside. On colder days, you can broil the tuna steaks inside, if desired.

SWEET ASIAN-GRILLED SALMON

Makes: 6 servings   Hands-On Time: 8 min.   Total Time: 14 min.

Brown sugar and hot mustard come together with soy sauce to make a "sweet-hot" glaze.

Vegetable cooking spray
1/4 cup Chinese hot mustard
3 Tbsp. dark brown sugar

1 Tbsp. soy sauce
1 tsp. rice vinegar
6 (6-oz.) skinless salmon fillets (1 1/4 inches thick)

1. Coat cold cooking grate with cooking spray and place on grill. Preheat grill to 350° to 400° (medium-high) heat. Whisk together mustard and next 3 ingredients in a bowl; reserve 1/3 cup to serve with cooked fillets. Brush half of remaining mustard mixture over 1 side of salmon.

2. Place fillets, mustard side down, on cooking grate. Grill, covered with grill lid, 4 minutes. Turn fillets over; brush with remaining half of mustard mixture. Grill, covered with grill lid, 2 minutes or to desired degree of doneness. Serve fillets with reserved mustard mixture.

PIT STOP

Oklahoma Joe's Barbecue

Kansas City, KS

This is my favorite barbecue joint in all the country! Set in an old gas station, the owners, Jeff and Joy Stehney, really know how to do barbecue right. They are part of the team "Slaughterhouse Five" and compete on the Kansas City Barbeque Society competition circuit. Jeff decided to go into the restaurant business after he and his team won numerous awards, such as Grand Champion for the American Royal Open, the Oklahoma State Championship, the World Brisket Open, and the Legend of the American Royal Award. You've got to try The Z-Man Sandwich—smoked beef brisket is topped with smoked provolone cheese and two crispy onion rings and served up on a Kaiser roll. Long live the Z-Man!

TERIYAKI-GLAZED GRILLED SALMON

Makes: 4 servings   Hands-On Time: 10 min.   Total Time: 10 min.

Jasmine rice and broccoli are ideal sides for these fillets seasoned with citrus juices, teriyaki sauce, and fresh ginger.

Citrus Teriyaki Glaze
Vegetable cooking spray
4   (6-oz.) salmon fillets

2   Tbsp. olive oil
1   tsp. kosher salt
1   tsp. coarsely ground pepper

1. Reserve ¼ cup glaze to serve with cooked salmon.

2. Coat cold cooking grate of grill with cooking spray, and place on grill. Preheat grill to 350° to 400° (medium-high) heat. Rub salmon with oil, and sprinkle with salt and pepper.

3. Grill, skin side up, covered with grill lid, 4 minutes. Turn salmon over; grill, covered with grill lid, 4 more minutes or to desired degree of doneness, basting often with remaining ½ cup glaze. Serve with reserved ¼ cup glaze.

CITRUS TERIYAKI GLAZE

Makes: ¾ cup   Hands-On Time: 27 min.   Total Time: 57 min.

Use this as a glaze for grilled vegetables, seafood, and chicken.

½   cup fresh orange juice
½   cup teriyaki sauce
¼   cup finely chopped green onions

3   Tbsp. fresh lime juice
2   Tbsp. minced fresh ginger
2   garlic cloves, minced

1. Stir together all ingredients in a small saucepan. Bring to a boil over medium-high heat, stirring often. Boil 10 minutes or until liquid is reduced by half. Remove from heat, and cool completely (about 30 minutes).

GRILLED SWORDFISH WITH OLIVE-BASIL RELISH

Makes: 4 servings   Hands-On Time: 26 min.   Total Time: 1 hour, 38 min., including relish

4   (8-oz.) swordfish steaks (1 inch thick)
Extra virgin olive oil
½ tsp. salt

½ tsp. ground white pepper
1   (3.5-oz.) bag boil-in-bag whole grain brown rice
Olive-Basil Relish

1. Preheat grill to 350° to 400° (medium-high) heat. Brush swordfish evenly with olive oil, and sprinkle with ½ tsp. salt and white pepper.

2. Grill swordfish, covered with grill lid, 4 to 5 minutes on each side or to desired degree of doneness. Remove from grill. Keep warm.

3. Prepare rice according to package directions. Place rice in a medium skillet, and stir in ⅔ cup Olive-Basil Relish. Cook over medium heat 1 minute or until thoroughly heated.

4. Divide rice mixture between 4 plates; top each with 1 swordfish steak. Spoon remaining Olive-Basil Relish over swordfish and rice mixture.

∾ HOW TO SEED A TOMATO ∾

OLIVE-BASIL RELISH

Makes: 1¾ cups
Hands-On Time: 12 min.
Total Time: 1 hour, 12 min.

- 2 plum tomatoes, seeded and finely diced
- ½ cup finely diced yellow bell pepper
- ¼ cup pitted kalamata olives, finely diced
- ¼ cup pitted green olives, finely diced
- ¼ cup finely diced red onion
- 2 Tbsp. drained small capers
- 1 Tbsp. chopped fresh basil leaves
- 1 garlic clove, minced
- ¼ cup extra virgin olive oil
- 2 tsp. sugar
- 1 tsp. red wine vinegar

Salt and freshly ground pepper to taste

1. Stir together first 8 ingredients in a large bowl.

2. Whisk together olive oil, sugar, and vinegar until blended. Pour over tomato mixture in bowl, and toss to coat. Cover and let stand at room temperature 1 hour. Season with salt and pepper to taste.

FISH KABOBS

Makes: 2 to 3 servings   Hands-On Time: 24 min.   Total Time: 54 min.

6   (6-inch) wooden skewers
1   (8-oz.) tuna fillet
1   (8-oz.) grouper fillet
1   (8-oz.) salmon fillet, skinned
1   (8-oz.) bottle olive oil-and-vinegar dressing

¼   cup chopped fresh flat-leaf parsley
1   Tbsp. fresh rosemary, chopped
1   Tbsp. pink peppercorns
2   Tbsp. lemon juice
Fresh herb sprigs (optional)

1. Soak skewers in water 30 minutes. Cut each fish fillet into 1-inch pieces. Thread fish onto skewers. Place kabobs in a shallow dish.

2. Stir together dressing and next 4 ingredients. Pour over fish; add fresh herb sprigs, if desired. Cover and chill 30 minutes.

3. Preheat grill to 400° to 500° (high) heat. Remove fish from marinade, discarding marinade. Grill, covered with grill lid, 4 minutes on each side or to desired degree of doneness.

CARIBBEAN SHRIMP KABOBS

Makes: 4 servings   Hands-On Time: 19 min.   Total Time: 49 min.

Perfect for entertaining, these quick and easy skewers are a breeze to make and offer just the right flavors for a summertime meal.

1   cup fresh orange juice
¼   cup fresh lime juice
¼   cup chopped fresh cilantro
¼   cup olive oil
½   tsp. salt
½   tsp. chili powder

4   garlic cloves, minced
1½ lb. peeled and deveined large raw shrimp
       with tails
4   (12-inch) metal or wooden skewers
Garnishes: orange slices, lime wedges

1. Whisk together first 7 ingredients in a large shallow dish or zip-top plastic freezer bag; add shrimp. Cover or seal, and chill 30 minutes. Preheat grill to 350° to 400° (medium-high) heat. Remove shrimp from marinade, reserving marinade. Thread shrimp onto skewers.

2. Grill shrimp, covered with grill lid, 2 minutes on each side or just until shrimp turn pink. Meanwhile, bring reserved marinade to a boil in a small saucepan, and cook 5 minutes. Remove from heat; drizzle over grilled shrimp. Garnish, if desired.

NOTE: If using wooden skewers, soak them in water for 30 minutes before assembling the kabobs.

HONEY-LIME GRILLED SHRIMP KABOBS

Makes: 3 servings   Hands-On Time: 16 min.   Total Time: 1 hour, 16 min.

Serve these kabobs with rice pilaf and mixed greens for an easy dinner.

1½ lb. unpeeled, jumbo raw shrimp
¼ cup extra virgin olive oil
2 Tbsp. minced fresh chives
2 Tbsp. fresh lime juice
2 Tbsp. rice vinegar
2 Tbsp. Dijon mustard

2 Tbsp. honey
1 tsp. kosher salt
½ tsp. garlic powder
½ tsp. freshly ground black pepper
¼ tsp. ground red pepper
3 (14-inch) metal skewers

1. Peel shrimp; devein, if desired. Whisk together oil and next 9 ingredients in a small bowl; reserve 3 Tbsp. for basting. Place remaining marinade in a large shallow dish or zip-top plastic freezer bag; add shrimp, turning to coat. Cover or seal, and chill 1 hour, turning once.

2. Preheat grill to 350° to 400° (medium-high) heat. Remove shrimp from marinade, discarding marinade. Thread shrimp onto 3 skewers, leaving a ¼-inch space between pieces. Grill, covered with grill lid, 3 minutes on each side or just until shrimp turn pink, basting with reserved 3 Tbsp. marinade.

HOW TO PEEL & DEVEIN SHRIMP

LEMONY HERB-GRILLED SCALLOPS

Makes: 4 servings   Hands-On Time: 19 min.   Total Time: 1 hour, 19 min.

For big impact, buy extra-large sea scallops to skewer. Then slather them hot-off-the-grill with homemade Citrus Butter.

⅓ cup olive oil
¼ cup fresh lemon juice (about 2 lemons)
1 Tbsp. chopped fresh basil
2 tsp. chopped fresh thyme
½ tsp. salt, divided

½ tsp. pepper, divided
2 garlic cloves, minced
12 extra-large sea scallops (1½ lb.)
4 (10-inch) metal skewers
Citrus Butter

1. Whisk together olive oil, lemon juice, herbs, ¼ tsp. salt, ¼ tsp. pepper, and garlic. Pour marinade into a zip-top plastic freezer bag; add scallops. Seal bag, and chill 1 hour.

2. Preheat grill to 350° to 400° (medium-high) heat. Remove scallops from marinade; discard marinade. Thread scallops onto skewers. Sprinkle scallops with remaining ¼ tsp. salt and pepper.

3. Grill scallops, covered with grill lid, 3 to 4 minutes on each side or just until scallops are opaque. Serve scallops with Citrus Butter.

CITRUS BUTTER

Makes: ½ cup   Hands-On Time: 5 min.   Total Time: 5 min.

Store any leftover flavored butter in the refrigerator. Use it on grilled chicken or fish.

½ cup butter, softened
1 tsp. lemon zest

1 tsp. lime zest
⅛ tsp. pepper

1. Stir together all ingredients in a small bowl. Cover and chill until ready to serve.

GRILLED SCALLOP KABOBS

Makes: 4 to 6 servings   Hands-On Time: 20 min.   Total Time: 20 min.

These easy skewers are perfect for any night of the week. Be sure to buy scallops equal in size so they'll cook evenly.

10 (6-inch) wooden skewers
20 fresh thick asparagus spears
10 sea scallops (about 1½ lb.)

¼ cup herb-flavored olive oil
Salt to taste
Lemon wedges

1. Soak wooden skewers in water 30 minutes. Meanwhile, preheat grill to 350° to 400° (medium-high) heat. Snap off and discard tough ends of asparagus. Cut asparagus into 2-inch pieces.

2. Thread scallops alternately with asparagus pieces onto skewers. Brush with olive oil.

3. Grill kabobs, covered with grill lid, 2½ minutes on each

side or just until scallops are opaque. Season with salt to taste. Serve kabobs with lemon wedges.

GRILLED OYSTERS WITH SPICY COCKTAIL SAUCE

Makes: 2 dozen   **Hands-On Time: 25 min.**   **Total Time: 25 min.**

2   dozen fresh oysters in the shell   Spicy Cocktail Sauce

1. Preheat grill to 300° to 350° (medium) heat. Place oysters in a single layer on grill grate.

2. Grill oysters, covered with grill lid, 20 minutes or until oysters open. Serve with Spicy Cocktail Sauce.

SPICY COCKTAIL SAUCE

Makes: about 4 cups   **Hands-On Time: 10 min.**   **Total Time: 10 min.**

Serve any remaining cocktail sauce with boiled shrimp or your favorite seafood.

1½ cups chili sauce
1   cup ketchup
¾   cup refrigerated horseradish
⅓   cup fresh lemon juice

1½ Tbsp. Worcestershire sauce
2   to 3 tsp. hot sauce
½   tsp. salt
½   tsp. pepper

1. Stir together all ingredients until blended. Cover and chill until ready to serve.

SPECIAL EXTRAS

GRILLED ROSEMARY LEMONADE

Makes: about 10 cups   **Hands-On Time: 54 min.**   **Total Time: 1 hour, 34 min.**

To get the right amount of juice for this recipe, buy large lemons. They are juicier than the small lemons in the bag.

10 large lemons
1½ cups sugar
4   (6-inch) rosemary sprigs

8   cups cold water
Garnish: rosemary sprigs

1. Grate zest from lemons to equal 1 Tbsp. Stir together zest, sugar, 4 rosemary sprigs, and 1½ cups water in a small saucepan. Bring to a boil over medium-high heat; reduce heat, and simmer, uncovered, 30 minutes or until reduced to 1¼ cups. Remove from heat; cool completely (about 30 minutes). Discard rosemary.

2. Preheat grill to 350° to 400° (medium-high) heat. Cut 10 lemons in half. Grill lemons, cut sides down, covered with grill lid, 7 minutes or until lightly browned. Remove lemons from grill; cool 10 minutes.

3. Cut each of 2 lemon halves into 5 wedges. Squeeze juice from

9 lemons into a measuring cup to equal 1½ cups. Stir together grilled lemon juice, rosemary syrup, and 8 cups cold water in a 3-qt. pitcher. Serve over ice with grilled lemon wedges; garnish, if desired.

NOTE: If you prefer sweeter lemonade, add additional sugar to pitcher.

RECIPE provided by Heath Hall of Pork Barrel BBQ.

TOMATO BRUSCHETTA

Makes: 8 servings   Hands-On Time: 17 min.   Total Time: 17 min.

16 (½-inch-thick) slices French bread baguette

3 Tbsp. extra virgin olive oil

4 ripe tomatoes, seeded and chopped

½ small sweet onion, thinly sliced

½ cup torn fresh basil

1 garlic clove, minced

½ tsp. kosher salt

¼ tsp. freshly ground pepper

1. Preheat grill to 350° to 400° (medium-high) heat. Brush both sides of bread with oil. Grill 1 to 1½ minutes per side or until toasted.

2. Toss together tomatoes and next 5 ingredients; serve over bread slices.

GRILLED VEGETABLE KABOBS

Makes: 4 servings   **Hands-On Time: 26 min.**   **Total Time: 4 hours, 26 min.**

These kabobs are a great way to use up some of your extra summer produce.

1   medium zucchini, cut into 1-inch pieces
1   sweet onion, cut into 1-inch wedges
16 fresh mushrooms

2   red bell peppers, cut into 2-inch squares
1   cup bottled balsamic vinaigrette
4   (14-inch) metal skewers

1. Place vegetables in a shallow dish or zip-top plastic freezer bag. Drizzle vinaigrette over vegetables, turning to coat. Cover or seal, and chill 4 hours and up to 24 hours.

2. Preheat grill to 350° to 400° (medium-high) heat.

3. Remove vegetables from marinade; discard marinade. Thread vegetables alternately onto skewers. Grill kabobs, covered with grill lid, 6 to 7 minutes on each side or until vegetables are crisp-tender and slightly charred.

GRILLED VEGETABLE RATATOUILLE

Makes: 12 servings   Hands-On Time: 41 min.   Total Time: 41 min.

Serve this Provençal vegetable blend as a side dish to grilled meats and chicken, or as a topping for pasta. Leftovers will hold several days in the fridge; just bring to room temperature before serving.

- 1   zucchini, quartered lengthwise
- 1   yellow squash, quartered lengthwise
- 1   eggplant, cut into ½-inch-thick slices
- 1   red onion, cut into ½-inch-thick slices
- 1   red bell pepper, quartered and seeded
- 1   yellow bell pepper, quartered and seeded
- 2   (8-oz.) packages baby portobello mushrooms
- 1   pt. cherry tomatoes
- ⅔   cup extra virgin olive oil, divided

- 2   Tbsp. Pork Barrel BBQ All-American Spice Rub or Sweet Melissa's BBQ Rub
- 6   (14-inch) metal skewers
- 2   Tbsp. balsamic vinegar
- ¼   cup fresh basil leaves, finely chopped
- 2   Tbsp. finely chopped fresh oregano
- ¾   tsp. salt
- 4   garlic cloves, minced

1. Preheat grill to 350° to 400° (medium-high) heat. Toss together vegetables and ½ cup oil in a large bowl. Sprinkle with rub, and toss to coat. Thread mushrooms and tomatoes onto skewers.

2. Grill cut vegetables, covered with grill lid, 4 minutes on each side or until tender. Grill skewered vegetables 4 minutes, turning occasionally.

3. Coarsely chop vegetables, and place in a large bowl. Add remaining oil, vinegar, basil, oregano, salt, and garlic; toss gently. Serve at room temperature.

RECIPE provided by Heath Hall of Pork Barrel BBQ.

GRILLED ROASTED PEPPER-STUFFED MUSHROOMS

Makes: 4 servings   Hands-On Time: 19 min.   Total Time: 34 min.

Look for mushrooms that are about 4 inches wide and have a raised rim around the edge of the gills to help contain the cheese mixture in the center.

4   portobello mushroom caps
1   large red bell pepper
1   small onion, cut into ½-inch-thick slices
1   (5.2-oz.) package buttery garlic-and-herb spreadable cheese

½   cup freshly grated Parmesan cheese
4   tsp. bottled balsamic glaze

1. Preheat grill to 400° to 450° (high) heat. Cut stem from mushrooms; chop stem, and reserve for cheese mixture. Scrape and discard brown gills from underside of mushrooms, leaving edges of caps intact, using a spoon.

2. Grill bell pepper, covered with grill lid, 15 minutes or until pepper looks blistered, turning often. At the same time, grill onion slices, covered with grill lid, 10 minutes or until crisp-tender.

3. Reduce grill temperature to medium heat. Remove bell pepper from grill, and place in a large zip-top plastic freezer bag; seal and let stand 10 minutes to loosen skin. Peel pepper; cut pepper in half. Remove and discard seeds. Chop bell pepper and onion slices.

4. Combine reserved chopped mushroom stems, chopped onion, and spreadable cheese.

5. Grill mushrooms, covered with grill lid, 5 minutes, turning once. Spoon cheese mixture into center of mushroom caps. Top each with chopped bell pepper and Parmesan cheese. Grill stuffed mushroom caps, covered with grill lid, 2 to 3 minutes or until mushrooms are tender and cheese mixture is bubbly around edges. Drizzle with balsamic glaze.

SWEET-GRILLED ZUCCHINI

Makes: 4 servings **Hands-On Time: 9 min.** **Total Time: 9 min.**

1 Tbsp. balsamic vinegar
1 Tbsp. olive oil
1 tsp. brown sugar
1 tsp. fresh lemon juice
½ tsp. kosher salt

½ tsp. minced garlic
¼ tsp. freshly ground black pepper
¼ tsp. dried crushed red pepper
2 medium zucchini, cut lengthwise into ¼-inch-thick slices

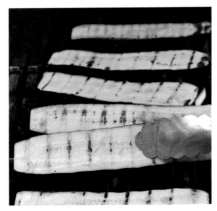

TROY'S TIP

Cutting the zucchini lengthwise makes it easier to grill. The long slices are a cinch to turn, and they don't fall through the cooking grate. Let the slices get slightly charred for best flavor.

1. Preheat grill to 350° to 400° (medium-high) heat. Whisk together first 8 ingredients in a small bowl. Brush mixture on both sides of zucchini.

2. Grill zucchini, covered with grill lid, 2 minutes on each side or until tender. Serve immediately.

KICKED-UP GRILLED ASPARAGUS

Makes: 6 servings   **Hands-On Time: 9 min.**   **Total Time: 9 min.**

Thick asparagus works best for this recipe. The trick to successful grilling is to place the stalks perpendicular to the rods on the grill rack so they don't fall through. Flip the stalks, several at a time, with tongs or a spatula.

1   **lb. fresh thick asparagus**
2   **Tbsp. olive oil**

1½ **tsp. Brisket Dry Rub (page 29)**

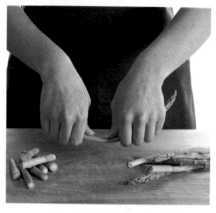

1. Preheat grill to 400° to 450° (high) heat. Snap off and discard tough ends of asparagus.

2. Place asparagus in a shallow baking dish. Drizzle with oil, and sprinkle with Brisket Dry Rub, tossing to coat.

3. Grill asparagus, covered with grill lid, 2 minutes or until crisp-tender.

GRILLED BOK CHOY

Makes: 6 servings　　**Hands-On Time: 9 min.**　　**Total Time: 9 min.**

Grill this simple veggie alongside fish or chicken to round out a meal.

¼   cup butter, melted
1   Tbsp. Pork Dry Rub (page 28)

2   garlic cloves, minced
6   heads baby bok choy, halved

1. Preheat grill to 350° to 400° (medium-high) heat. Stir together butter, Pork Dry Rub, and garlic in a small bowl.

2. Grill bok choy, covered with grill lid, 2 minutes on each side or until edges are slightly charred, basting often with butter mixture.

PIT STOP

Grady's Barbecue
Dudley, NC

This Eastern North Carolina legend is a real joint. Gerri and Steve Grady opened their doors for business on July 4, 1986, when Gerri was out of work due to an injury. Because Steve had access to wood from a previous employer, they began cooking their barbecue the traditional Eastern Carolina way over open pits and do so to this day.

Like others in this region of the barbecue belt, they believe in whole hog barbecue where the whole pig is smoked over an open wood fire, chopped finely, and then drenched in a red pepper flake-and-cider vinegar sauce. Although this restaurant is hard to find (you'll miss it if you blink), it's definitely worth a U-turn. They serve up home-cooked favorites like black-eyed peas, collards, and hush puppies alongside the smoky pork.

GRILLED ARTICHOKES

Makes: 8 servings   Hands-On Time: 32 min.   Total Time: 52 min.

4   artichokes
2   lemons, halved
¾   cup olive oil
1   tsp. kosher salt

½   tsp. freshly ground pepper
4   garlic cloves, minced
¼   cup freshly grated Parmesan cheese

1. Wash artichokes by plunging in cold water. Cut off stem ends, and trim about ½ inch from top of each artichoke. Remove any loose bottom leaves.

2. Trim one-fourth off top of each outer leaf with scissors. Cut each artichoke in half lengthwise. Rub edges with cut lemons, reserving lemons.

3. Remove thistle with a spoon. Fill a 12-qt. stockpot with 4 inches water; bring to a boil over high heat. Add artichokes; cover and cook 20 minutes or just until barely tender.

4. Preheat grill to 350° to 400° (medium-high) heat. Whisk together oil, salt, pepper, and garlic. Grill, cut sides down, covered with grill lid, 6 minutes. Turn; spoon olive oil mixture over artichoke halves.

5. Grill, covered with grill lid, 6 more minutes or until slightly charred and lower leaves pull out easily. At same time, grill lemons, cut sides down, covered with lid, 5 minutes or until slightly charred.

6. Place artichokes, cut sides up, on a serving platter; squeeze grilled lemons over artichokes, and sprinkle with Parmesan cheese.

CHIPOTLE-CILANTRO SLAW

Makes: 6 to 8 servings   Hands-On Time: 15 min.   Total Time: 15 min.

¼ cup mayonnaise
1   Tbsp. sugar
2   Tbsp. sour cream
1   tsp. lime zest
2   Tbsp. fresh lime juice
2   tsp. red wine vinegar
½ tsp. salt

½ tsp. pepper
1   (16-oz.) package shredded coleslaw mix
1   carrot, shredded
2   canned chipotle chile peppers in adobo sauce, finely chopped
½ cup minced fresh cilantro

1. Whisk together first 8 ingredients in a large bowl. Add coleslaw mix and remaining ingredients, and stir until coated. Serve immediately, or cover and chill up to 1 hour.

⤙ HOW TO PEEL & GRATE CARROTS ⤚

GRILLED GREEN TOMATOES CAPRESE

Makes: 8 to 10 servings   **Hands-On Time: 21 min.**   **Total Time: 1 hour, 21 min.**

Using white (rather than brown) balsamic vinegar in the marinade brightens the color of the grilled tomatoes, but the salad's flavor is extraordinary with either.

½ cup olive oil
¼ cup white balsamic vinegar
2 garlic cloves, minced
1 Tbsp. brown sugar
⅛ tsp. salt
4 medium-size green tomatoes, cut into ¼-inch-thick slices (about 2 lb.)

1 (16-oz.) package sliced fresh mozzarella cheese
Kosher salt and freshly ground pepper to taste
⅓ cup small fresh basil leaves

1. Combine first 5 ingredients in a large zip-top plastic freezer bag; add tomatoes, seal, and shake gently to coat. Chill 1 hour.

2. Preheat grill to 350° to 400° (medium-high) heat. Remove tomatoes from marinade, reserving marinade. Grill tomatoes, covered with grill lid, 3 to 4 minutes on each side or until tender and grill marks appear.

3. Arrange alternating slices of warm grilled tomatoes and mozzarella cheese on a large, shallow platter. Drizzle with reserved marinade; season with salt and pepper to taste. Sprinkle with basil.

BLACK-EYED PEAS

Makes: 6 to 8 servings   Hands-On Time: 5 min.   Total Time: 10 hours, 18 min.

It's hard to improve upon a pot of long-simmered peas. Here, we recommend adding a pinch of garlic powder or dried crushed red pepper.

1   (16-oz.) package dried black-eyed peas
½   lb. smoked ham hocks
1   large yellow onion, chopped

½   tsp. freshly ground pepper
2   tsp. salt

1. Rinse and sort peas according to package directions. Place peas in a Dutch oven. Cover with water 2 inches above peas; let soak 8 hours. Drain. Place peas in a 6-qt. stockpot. Add ham hocks, onion, pepper, and ½ gal. water.

2. Bring to a boil over medium-high heat. Cover, reduce heat, and simmer 2 hours or until peas are tender, adding salt the last 30 minutes of cooking.

RECIPE provided by Ed Mitchell.

COLLARD GREENS

Makes: 6 to 8 servings   Hands-On Time: 1 hour, 40 min.   Total Time: 3 hours, 14 min.

Shop for meaty ham hocks that will impart an abundance of smoky flavor to the greens. And don't forget to put some pepper sauce on the table for serving.

3   lb. smoked ham hocks
3   lb. fresh collard greens, trimmed and chopped
1   large onion, chopped

¼   cup white vinegar
1   Tbsp. salt
½   tsp. freshly ground pepper

1. Bring 1½ gal. water to a boil in a 12-qt. stockpot. Add ham hocks. Reduce heat to low, and simmer, uncovered, 1 hour. Remove ham hocks; chop meat. Return meat to cooking liquid.

2. Add collards, onion, vinegar, salt, and pepper. Cook, uncovered, stirring occasionally, 1 hour and 30 minutes or to desired degree of tenderness.

RECIPE provided by Ed Mitchell.

CHIPOTLE GRILLED CORN

Makes: 8 servings
Hands-On Time: 36 min.
Total Time: 36 min.

Serve six ears of corn hot off the grill, and save two ears of buttered corn to make Black Bean and Grilled Corn Salad (page 253).

$\frac{1}{2}$ cup unsalted butter, melted
2   Tbsp. chipotle hot sauce
1   Tbsp. fresh lime juice
Vegetable cooking spray
8   ears fresh corn, husks removed
$\frac{1}{2}$ tsp. kosher salt
$\frac{1}{4}$ tsp. coarsely ground pepper

1. Preheat grill to 350° to 400° (medium-high) heat. Stir together butter, hot sauce, and lime juice in a bowl.

2. Lightly coat corn with cooking spray. Grill corn, covered with grill lid, 15 to 20 minutes or until tender, turning every 5 minutes. Brush corn evenly with butter mixture; sprinkle with salt and pepper.

BLACK BEAN AND GRILLED CORN SALAD

Makes: 6 servings   **Hands-On Time: 8 min.**   **Total Time: 8 min.**

¼ cup cider vinegar
3 Tbsp. chopped fresh cilantro
2 Tbsp. canola oil
½ tsp. salt
½ tsp. sugar

½ tsp. coarsely ground pepper
½ tsp. ground cumin
½ tsp. chili powder
1 (15-oz.) can black beans, drained and rinsed
2 ears Chipotle Grilled Corn (page 251)

1. Whisk together first 8 ingredients in a medium bowl. Add black beans, tossing to coat.

2. Cut kernels from cobs; discard cobs. Add kernels to salad, tossing to coat.

SWEET POTATOES ON THE GRILL

Makes: 4 servings   **Hands-On Time: 12 min.**   **Total Time: 42 min.**

2 (8-oz.) sweet potatoes, peeled and cut into ¼-inch-thick slices
3 Tbsp. butter, cut into pieces

½ cup firmly packed brown sugar
½ tsp. ground cinnamon

1. Preheat grill to 300° to 350° (medium) heat.

2. Place sweet potatoes on a lightly greased 24- x 18-inch piece of heavy-duty aluminum foil; dot with butter, and sprinkle with brown sugar and cinnamon. Fold foil to seal.

3. Grill, covered with grill lid, 30 minutes or until sweet potatoes are tender, turning packet over after 15 minutes.

GRILLED SWEET POTATO PLANKS

Makes: 6 servings   **Hands-On Time: 20 min.**   **Total Time: 20 min.**

⅓ cup olive oil
1 Tbsp. minced shallot
1 Tbsp. chopped fresh rosemary
1 tsp. kosher salt

1 tsp. coarsely ground pepper
3 large sweet potatoes, peeled and cut into ¼-inch-thick slices
½ cup crumbled blue cheese

1. Preheat grill to 350° to 400° (medium-high) heat. Stir together first 5 ingredients in a small bowl. Brush olive oil mixture over sweet potato slices.

2. Grill, covered with grill lid, 3 to 4 minutes on each side or until tender. Place potatoes on a serving platter; sprinkle with blue cheese.

HOW TO PEEL, SLICE & MINCE SHALLOTS

GRILLED FINGERLING POTATO SALAD

Makes: 8 servings   Hands-On Time: 20 min.   Total Time: 3 hours, including vinaigrette and shallots

6   cups fingerling potatoes (about 3 lb.), halved
     lengthwise
2   Tbsp. extra virgin olive oil
1   tsp. kosher salt
½   tsp. freshly ground pepper
3   Tbsp. Whole Grain Mustard Vinaigrette

3   Tbsp. Pickled Shallots
2   Tbsp. chopped fresh chives
2   Tbsp. chopped fresh flat-leaf parsley
1   tsp. chopped fresh thyme
3   Tbsp. cooked and crumbled bacon (optional)

1. Preheat grill to 350° to 400° (medium-high) heat. Toss potatoes with olive oil; sprinkle with salt and pepper. Place, cut sides down, on cooking grate; grill, covered with grill lid, 2 minutes or until grill marks appear.

2. Remove from grill. Place potatoes in a single layer in center of a large piece of heavy-duty aluminum foil. Bring up foil sides over potatoes; double fold top and side edges to seal, making a packet. Grill potatoes, in foil packet, covered with grill lid, 15 minutes on each side.

3. Remove packet from grill. Carefully open packet, using tongs. Cool 5 minutes. Toss together potatoes, vinaigrette, next 4 ingredients, and, if desired, bacon.

WHOLE GRAIN MUSTARD VINAIGRETTE

Makes: $2/3$ **cup**

1/4 cup white wine vinegar
1 Tbsp. light brown sugar
3 Tbsp. whole grain mustard

1/2 tsp. freshly ground pepper
1/8 tsp. salt
1/3 cup olive oil

1. Whisk together vinegar, brown sugar, mustard, pepper, and salt. Add olive oil in a slow, steady stream, whisking constantly until smooth.

PICKLED SHALLOTS

Makes: $1\frac{1}{2}$ **cups**

3/4 cup red wine vinegar
1/3 cup sugar
2 Tbsp. kosher salt

1/2 tsp. dried crushed red pepper
1 1/2 cups thinly sliced shallots

1. Bring 3/4 cup water, vinegar, sugar, salt, and crushed red pepper to a boil, whisking until sugar and salt are dissolved. Pour over shallots in a hot, sterilized canning jar. Cool to room temperature. Cover and chill 1 hour.

TROY'S TIP

Save time by prepping ahead. Make the vinaigrette and pickled shallots the day before.

FRESH HERB POTATO SALAD

Makes: 10 to 12 servings   **Hands-On Time: 30 min.**   **Total Time: 1 hour, 15 min.**

4   lb. Yukon gold potatoes
½   cup diced celery
½   cup chopped fresh flat-leaf parsley
⅓   cup finely chopped green onions
3   hard-cooked eggs, peeled and grated
1   cup mayonnaise

½   cup sour cream
3   Tbsp. chopped fresh tarragon
2   garlic cloves, pressed
1   Tbsp. Dijon mustard
1   tsp. salt
¾   tsp. freshly ground pepper

1. Cook potatoes in boiling water to cover 30 to 40 minutes or until tender; drain and cool 15 minutes. Peel potatoes; cut into 1-inch cubes.

2. Stir together potatoes, celery, parsley, green onions, and eggs in a large bowl.

3. Stir together mayonnaise and next 6 ingredients; stir into potato mixture. Serve immediately, or cover and chill up to 12 hours.

TROY'S TIP

Allowing the potatoes to cool prevents them from becoming mushy after the creamy dressing is added.

3-BEAN BBQ BAKED BEANS

Makes: 8 to 10 servings   **Hands-On Time: 2 hours, 34 min.**   **Total Time: 11 hours, 19 min.**

¾ **cup dried pinto beans**
1 **cup dried red kidney beans**
¾ **cup dried black beans**
½ **lb. bacon slices**
½ **lb. ground pork sausage**

½ **cup diced yellow onion**
⅔ **cup firmly packed dark brown sugar**
1½ **Tbsp. yellow mustard**
1 **tsp. salt**

1. Place beans in a large stockpot; cover with water 2 inches above beans. Let soak 8 hours. Drain. Bring beans and 10 cups water to a boil in stockpot. Partially cover, reduce heat, and simmer 2 hours or until beans are tender, stirring occasionally. (Do not drain beans.)

2. Preheat oven to 350°. Cook bacon in a large skillet over medium-high heat 4 minutes or until crisp; remove bacon, and drain on paper towels, reserving drippings in skillet. Crumble bacon. Add sausage and onion to hot drippings in skillet; cook over medium-high heat, stirring often, 4 minutes or until sausage crumbles and is no

3. Stir ½ cup water, brown sugar, mustard, and salt into beans. Add bacon and sausage mixture, stirring until blended. Pour bean mixture into an 11- x 7-inch baking dish. Bake, covered, at 350° for 45 minutes or until bubbly.

RECIPE provided by Ed Mitchell.

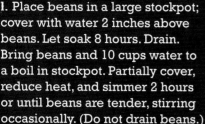

DAVENPORT RANCH COWBOY BAKED BEANS

Makes: 6 servings   **Hands-On Time: 15 min.**   **Total Time: 1 hour**

Canned baked beans get a boost of extra flavor with smoky bacon, tangy mustard, and sweet brown sugar.

- 3   bacon slices
- 1   medium-size yellow onion, finely chopped
- 1   (28-oz.) can baked beans
- ¼   cup firmly packed light brown sugar
- 2   Tbsp. molasses
- 2   Tbsp. yellow mustard

1. Preheat oven to 400°. Cook bacon in a large skillet over medium-high heat 5 to 6 minutes or until crisp; remove bacon, and drain on paper towels, reserving 2 Tbsp. drippings in skillet. Crumble bacon.

2. Sauté onion in hot drippings over medium heat 5 minutes or until tender. Stir together onion, crumbled bacon, beans, and remaining ingredients in a lightly greased 2-qt. baking dish.

3. Bake at 400° for 45 minutes or until thickened and bubbly.

RECIPE provided by Nicole Davenport.

TROY'S TIP

This recipe can easily be doubled to feed a crowd.

CLASSIC BAKED MACARONI AND CHEESE

Makes: 6 to 8 servings   Hands-On Time: 27 min.   Total Time: 47 min.

This is the ultimate side dish to serve with your favorite BBQ.

2   cups milk
2   Tbsp. butter
2   Tbsp. all-purpose flour
½   tsp. salt
¼   tsp. freshly ground black pepper

1   (10-oz.) block extra-sharp Cheddar cheese, shredded
¼   tsp. ground red pepper (optional)
½   (16-oz.) package elbow macaroni, cooked

1. Preheat oven to 400°. Microwave milk at HIGH 1½ minutes. Melt butter in a large skillet or Dutch oven over medium-low heat; whisk in flour until smooth. Cook, whisking constantly, 1 minute.

2. Gradually whisk in warm milk, and cook, whisking constantly, 5 minutes or until thickened.

3. Whisk in salt, black pepper, 1 cup shredded cheese, and, if desired, red pepper until smooth; stir in pasta. Spoon pasta mixture into a lightly greased 2-qt. baking dish; top with remaining cheese. Bake at 400° for 20 minutes or until golden and bubbly.

NOTE: We tested with Cracker Barrel Extra-Sharp Cheddar.

TROY'S TIP

To ensure a lump-free sauce, whisk warm milk into the flour mixture. I also recommend shredding your own cheese for a creamier texture.

Chipotle-Cilantro
Slaw (page 245)

Sweet, Salty, and Spicy
Watermelon Refresher
(page 269)

**Chipotle-Bacon
Mac and Cheese
(page 268)**

**Tangy Tzatziki Pasta Salad
(page 269)**

CHIPOTLE-BACON MAC AND CHEESE

Makes: 10 servings   Hands-On Time: 40 min.   Total Time: 1 hour, 20 min.

- 3   tsp. sea salt, divided
- 1   (16-oz.) package cavatappi pasta
- 2   Tbsp. corn oil, divided
- ½   cup butter
- 1   small onion, diced
- 3   Tbsp. all-purpose flour
- 3   cups half-and-half
- 2   cups heavy cream
- 1   tsp. ground white pepper
- 3   cups (12 oz.) freshly grated smoked Cheddar cheese
- 1   cup (4 oz.) freshly grated Cheddar cheese
- 1   tsp. ground chipotle chile pepper
- 6   cooked bacon slices, chopped
- ¾   cup panko (Japanese breadcrumbs)

1. Preheat oven to 350°. Bring 1 gal. water and 1½ tsp. salt to a boil in a Dutch oven; add pasta. Cook 8 to 9 minutes or until al dente. Drain; rinse with cold water. Toss with 1 Tbsp. oil.

2. Melt butter in a large saucepan over medium-high heat. Add onion, and sauté 4 to 5 minutes or until tender. Add flour, and cook, whisking constantly, 1 to 2 minutes or until smooth. (Do not brown flour.) Add half-and-half, next 2 ingredients, and remaining 1½ tsp. sea salt, and bring to a simmer. Cook, whisking constantly, 5 to 6 minutes or until thickened. Gradually add cheeses, stirring until blended. Transfer mixture to a large bowl; stir in cooked pasta. Spoon into a lightly greased 13- x 9-inch baking dish.

3. Sauté chipotle pepper in remaining 1 Tbsp. hot corn oil in a small skillet over medium heat 30 seconds or until mixture begins to smoke. Remove from heat, and quickly stir in bacon and panko until coated. Sprinkle mixture over pasta.

4. Bake at 350° for 15 to 20 minutes or until golden and crisp on top. Serve immediately.

TROY'S TIP

It's very important to cook the pasta in salted water. The salt is absorbed and creates the perfect balance of saltiness when combined with the other ingredients.

TANGY TZATZIKI PASTA SALAD

Makes: 10 servings   Hands-On Time: 35 min.   Total Time: 2 hours, 35 min.

1   (16-oz.) container plain low-fat Greek yogurt
¼   cup olive oil
1   Tbsp. chopped fresh dill
1   Tbsp. fresh lemon juice
1   tsp. sea salt
½   tsp. freshly ground pepper
3   garlic cloves
1   (16-oz.) package penne pasta

1   cup pitted kalamata olives, sliced
2   cucumbers, peeled, seeded, and diced
¾   cup sun-dried tomatoes in oil, drained and chopped
1   (9.9-oz.) jar marinated artichoke hearts, drained and chopped
1½ cups crumbled feta cheese

1. Process first 7 ingredients in a food processor 30 seconds or until thoroughly blended. Transfer to a bowl, and cover and chill 1 to 24 hours.

2. Cook pasta according to package directions; drain and rinse with cold water.

3. Place cooled pasta in a large bowl. Stir in olives and next 3 ingredients until well blended. Add yogurt mixture, and stir just until well coated. Gently stir in feta cheese. Cover and chill 1 hour.

SWEET, SALTY, AND SPICY WATERMELON REFRESHER

Makes: 10 to 12 servings   Hands-On Time: 30 min.   Total Time: 50 min.

¼   cup fresh lime juice
1   Tbsp. turbinado sugar
2   Tbsp. fresh orange juice
1   jalapeño or 2 serrano peppers, seeded and minced
½   tsp. sea or kosher salt
¼   tsp. dried crushed red pepper
1   small red onion, diced

½   cup coarsely chopped fresh cilantro
2   Tbsp. coarsely chopped fresh mint
1   small seedless watermelon
1   small cantaloupe
2   English cucumbers
1   jicama
2   mangoes
Salt and pepper to taste

1. Combine lime juice and next 5 ingredients.

2. Place red onion, cilantro, and mint in a large bowl. Dice watermelon and cantaloupe into 1-inch pieces; add to bowl. Peel and dice cucumbers, jicama, and mangoes; add to bowl. Stir in lime juice mixture. Cover and chill 20 minutes. Add salt and pepper to taste.

HUSH PUPPIES

Makes: 8 to 10 servings (about 2 dozen hush puppies)   Hands-On Time: 25 min.   Total Time: 35 min.

Vegetable oil
1½ cups self-rising white cornmeal mix
¾ cup self-rising flour
¾ cup diced sweet onion (about ½ medium onion)

1½ Tbsp. sugar
1   large egg, lightly beaten
1¼ cups buttermilk

1. Pour oil to depth of 3 inches into a Dutch oven; heat to 375°. Combine cornmeal mix and next 3 ingredients. Add egg and buttermilk; stir just until moistened. Let stand 10 minutes.

2. Drop batter by tablespoonfuls into hot oil; fry, in 3 batches, 2 to 3 minutes on each side or until golden. Keep warm in a 200° oven.

~ TRY THESE TWISTS ~

BACON-AND-CARAMELIZED ONION HUSH PUPPIES (PICTURED): Increase onion to 1½ cups. Cook 5 bacon slices in a medium skillet over medium heat 5 to 6 minutes or until crisp; drain bacon on paper towels, reserving 2 Tbsp. drippings in skillet. Crumble bacon. Sauté onion in hot drippings over medium-low heat 12 to 15 minutes or until golden brown. Proceed with recipe as directed, stirring in onion and bacon with cornmeal mix in Step 2.

JALAPEÑO-PINEAPPLE HUSH PUPPIES: Prepare recipe as directed, stirring in ½ cup canned pineapple tidbits and 2 to 3 Tbsp. seeded and diced jalapeño pepper with cornmeal mix in Step 2.

SHRIMP-AND-CORN HUSH PUPPIES: Prepare recipe as directed, reducing buttermilk to ¾ cup and stirring 1½ cups chopped cooked shrimp (about ¾ lb. peeled) and 1 (8¾-oz.) can cream-style corn into batter in Step 2.

GRILLED PEACHES WITH WHIPPED CREAM AND RASPBERRY-MINT MASH

Makes: 4 servings   **Hands-On Time: 14 min.**   **Total Time: 14 min.**

Enjoy summer peaches warm from the grill in this fruit dessert that's reminiscent of the classic Peach Melba.

2   **cups fresh raspberries**
2   **Tbsp. chopped fresh mint**
4   **peaches, halved**
2   **Tbsp. canola oil**

4   **tsp. light brown sugar**
Sweetened whipped cream
Garnishes: raspberries, chopped fresh mint
       leaves, milk chocolate curls

1. Preheat grill to 350° to 400° (medium-high) heat. Place raspberries in a bowl; mash with a fork or potato masher just until chunky. Stir in mint.

2. Brush cut sides of peach halves with oil, and sprinkle with brown sugar. Grill, cut sides down, covered with grill lid, 4 minutes. Turn peaches over; grill 1 more minute or until tender.

3. Spoon raspberry mixture into the cavity of each peach half; top with whipped cream. Garnish, if desired.

RECIPE provided by Heath Hall of Pork Barrel BBQ.

SUMMER FRUIT COBBLER

Makes: 6 to 8 servings   Hands-On Time: 20 min.   Total Time: 1 hour, 25 min.

3   Tbsp. cornstarch
1½ cups sugar, divided
3   cups coarsely chopped, peeled fresh
    nectarines
2   cups fresh blueberries
1   cup fresh raspberries

½   cup butter, softened
2   large eggs
1½ cups all-purpose flour
1½ tsp. baking powder
1   (8-oz.) container sour cream
½   tsp. baking soda

1. Preheat oven to 350°. Stir together cornstarch and ½ cup sugar. Toss nectarines and berries with cornstarch mixture, and spoon into a lightly greased 11- x 7-inch baking dish.

2. Beat butter at medium speed with an electric mixer until fluffy; gradually add remaining 1 cup sugar, beating well. Add eggs, 1 at a time, beating just until blended after each addition.

3. Combine flour and baking powder. Stir together sour cream and baking soda. Add flour mixture to butter mixture alternately with sour cream mixture, beginning and ending with flour mixture. Beat at low speed just until blended after each addition. Spoon batter over fruit mixture.

4. Bake at 350° for 45 minutes; shield loosely with aluminum foil to prevent excessive browning; bake 20 to 25 more minutes or until a wooden pick inserted in center comes out clean.

PECAN PIE BARS

Makes: 36 servings **Hands-On Time: 15 min.** **Total Time: 2 hours, 55 min.**

These bars have a very crisp, sugary crust, making them ideal for make-ahead.

3 cups all-purpose flour
1 cup granulated sugar
¼ tsp. salt
¾ cup cold butter, cut up
1½ cups light corn syrup

1 cup firmly packed light brown sugar
¼ cup butter
4 large eggs, lightly beaten
2½ cups coarsely chopped pecans
1 tsp. vanilla

1. Preheat oven to 350°. Whisk together flour, granulated sugar, and salt in a large bowl. Cut cold butter into flour mixture with a pastry blender or fork until crumbly. Press mixture into bottom of a well-greased 15- x 10-inch jelly-roll pan. Bake at 350° for 17 to 20 minutes or until edges are light golden brown.

2. Combine corn syrup, brown sugar, and ¼ cup butter in a medium saucepan; bring to a boil, whisking to dissolve sugar. Cool 5 minutes. Whisk eggs in a large bowl. Gradually whisk half of hot syrup mixture into eggs; gradually whisk egg mixture into hot syrup mixture, whisking constantly. Stir in pecans and vanilla. Spread

pecan mixture over crust. Bake at 350° for 20 minutes or until set. Cool completely on a wire rack (about 2 hours). Cut into 36 squares.

RECIPE provided by Nicole Davenport.

TROY'S TIP

Make sure the butter is cold when you blend it into the flour. The crust will bake up to crispy perfection.

SWEET POTATO FLUFF

Makes: 8 servings   **Hands-On Time: 10 min.**   **Total Time: 55 min.**

"This is my mother's recipe. It was always on the table at Thanksgiving, as well as Christmas. The note on the card said 'double for holidays.' It was not considered a dessert, but I always thought it was when I was a child. I even remember eating this as leftovers late at night with a little ice cream on top. Awesome."

4   cups mashed cooked sweet potatoes
1⅓ cups granulated sugar
⅔   cup butter, melted
1½ tsp. vanilla extract
3   large eggs

1⅓ cups firmly packed light brown sugar
⅔   cup all-purpose flour
⅔   cup chopped pecans
⅓   cup butter, softened

1. Preheat oven to 350°. Beat first 5 ingredients at medium speed with an electric mixer until smooth. Spoon mixture into a lightly greased 11- x 7-inch baking dish.

2. Stir together brown sugar and remaining 3 ingredients with a fork until mixture is crumbly. Sprinkle over sweet potato mixture. Bake at 350° for 45 minutes or until browned and bubbly.

RECIPE provided by Sam Jones of the Skylight Inn.

TROY'S TIP

To get perfectly cooked sweet potatoes for the 4 cups of mashed potatoes, you'll need to start with about 3 lb. sweet potatoes. Bake them at 400° for 45 minutes to an hour.

BISCUIT PUDDING

Makes: 12 servings
Hands-On Time: 35 min.   **Total Time:** 1 hour, 40 min.

"This one is super special to me. It's my grandmother's recipe for her 'biscuit pudding,' which had an amazing chocolate dressing that I believe may have had healing power! The recipe stands out to me because it kind of got me in a little trouble when I was young. We would go to my grandparents every Sunday night after church and have leftovers from Sunday dinner. I loved this pudding to the point that it was sinful. My grandmother would always cut out a huge square for me to take home. One Monday, I took this to school, and when I started to eat it, a classmate asked if he could have some. My reply: sure, for 50 cents! I sold my pudding, made two bucks, and got reprimanded by my teacher! My parents were informed of my money-making scheme. This dish is still my favorite."

Biscuit Pudding
3   (9.5-oz.) cans refrigerated
    butter-me-not biscuits
4   cups milk
3½ cups sugar
1   cup butter, melted
1   tsp. vanilla extract
½   tsp. ground nutmeg

5   large eggs
Chocolate Topping
1½ cups sugar
⅓   cup unsweetened cocoa
3   Tbsp. all-purpose flour
2   cups milk
2   Tbsp. butter

1. Prepare Biscuit Pudding: Bake biscuits according to package directions. Remove from oven, and let cool.

2. Reduce oven temperature to 350°. Combine milk and next 5 ingredients in a 4-qt. bowl; beat at medium speed with an electric mixer until well blended. Crumble biscuits into milk mixture; beat just until blended. Transfer mixture to a lightly greased 13- x 9-inch pan.

3. Bake at 350° for 1 hour and 5 minutes or until golden and set.

4. Prepare Chocolate Topping: Whisk together sugar, cocoa, and flour in a medium saucepan; gradually whisk in milk. Cook over medium heat, stirring constantly, 16 minutes or until mixture boils and thickens. Remove from heat; add butter, stirring to melt. Serve over warm pudding.

RECIPE provided by Sam Jones of the Skylight Inn.

"And what about the sauce? There isn't any."

Sam Jones
Skylight Inn
Ayden, NC

In 1947, Pete Jones, also known as "The King of Barbecue," opened the Skylight Inn in Eastern North Carolina. This slice of the barbecue belt specializes in whole hog barbecue, and Pete made sure he stuck to that 180-year-old tradition. Now, "nose to tail" cooking is somewhat of a trend. But Pete has been cooking that way ever since he was 17 and learned the trade from his extended family (the Dennis's who were the first in North Carolina to serve pit barbecue to locals).

Sam Jones, Pete's grandson, now runs the family business and is not changing the way they make BBQ anytime soon. The whole hog is smoked over oak wood logs in the barbecue pit behind the restaurant. The hog is cooked until the meat is perfectly tender and the skin is crispy. No need for thermometers; doneness is determined by feel. Then, everything gets chopped up by hand—a cleaver in each to create a mountain of pork perfection. And what about the sauce? There isn't any. Just a dousing of vinegar and a little hot sauce highlights a perfectly smoky, succulent pork sandwich or barbecue plate.

BANANA PUDDING

Makes: 16 servings **Hands-On Time: 40 min.** **Total Time: 1 hour, 25 min.**

6 egg whites
1 tsp. cream of tartar
1 cup sugar
4 (3.4-oz.) packages vanilla cook-and-serve
   pudding mix

8 cups milk
1 (14-oz.) can sweetened condensed milk
1 (11-oz.) box vanilla wafers
5 large bananas, sliced

1. Preheat oven to 375°. Beat egg whites and cream of tartar at high speed with an electric mixer until foamy. Gradually add sugar, 1 Tbsp. at a time, beating until stiff peaks form and sugar dissolves.

2. Stir together pudding mix and milks in a large saucepan. Bring to a full boil over medium heat, stirring constantly.

3. Spread half of hot pudding into a 13- x 9-inch baking dish (cover remaining pudding and keep warm); quickly arrange vanilla wafers and banana slices, slightly overlapping, over pudding. Spread remaining half of hot pudding over bananas.

4. Spread meringue over hot pudding, sealing edges.

5. Bake at 375° for 15 minutes or until meringue is golden brown. Remove from oven, and let stand 30 minutes before serving.

RECIPE provided by Ed Mitchell.

HOW TO WHIP EGG WHITES TO STIFF PEAKS

METRIC EQUIVALENTS

The information in the following charts is provided to help cooks outside the United States successfully use the recipes in this book. All equivalents are approximate.

EQUIVALENTS FOR DIFFERENT TYPES OF INGREDIENTS

Standard Cup	Fine Powder (ex. flour)	Grain (ex. rice)	Granular (ex. sugar)	Liquid Solids (ex. butter)	Liquid (ex. milk)
1	140 g	150 g	190 g	200 g	240 ml
¾	105 g	113 g	143 g	150 g	180 ml
⅔	93 g	100 g	125 g	133 g	160 ml
½	70 g	75 g	95 g	100 g	120 ml
⅓	47 g	50 g	63 g	67 g	80 ml
¼	35 g	38 g	48 g	50 g	60 ml
⅛	18 g	19 g	24 g	25 g	30 ml

DRY INGREDIENTS BY WEIGHT

(To convert ounces to grams, multiply the number of ounces by 30.)

1 oz	=	1/16 lb	=	30 g
4 oz	=	¼ lb	=	120 g
8 oz	=	½ lb	=	240 g
12 oz	=	¾ lb	=	360 g
16 oz	=	1 lb	=	480 g

LENGTH

(To convert inches to centimeters, multiply the number of inches by 2.5.)

1 in				=	2.5 cm		
6 in	=	½ ft	=		15 cm		
12 in	=	1 ft	=		30 cm		
36 in	=	3 ft	=	1 yd	=	90 cm	
40 in				=	100 cm	=	1 m

LIQUID INGREDIENTS BY VOLUME

¼ tsp	=					1 ml
½ tsp	=					2 ml
1 tsp	=					5 ml
3 tsp	=	1 Tbsp	=		½ fl oz	=	15 ml
		2 Tbsp	=	⅛ cup	=	1 fl oz	=	30 ml
		4 Tbsp	=	¼ cup	=	2 fl oz	=	60 ml
		5⅓ Tbsp	=	⅓ cup	=	3 fl oz	=	80 ml
		8 Tbsp	=	½ cup	=	4 fl oz	=	120 ml
		10⅔ Tbsp	=	⅔ cup	=	5 fl oz	=	160 ml
		12 Tbsp	=	¾ cup	=	6 fl oz	=	180 ml
		16 Tbsp	=	1 cup	=	8 fl oz	=	240 ml
		1 pt	=	2 cups	=	16 fl oz	=	480 ml
		1 qt	=	4 cups	=	32 fl oz	=	960 ml
						33 fl oz	=	1000 ml	=	1 l

COOKING/OVEN TEMPERATURES

	Fahrenheit	Celsius	Gas Mark
Freeze Water	32° F	0° C	
Room Temperature	68° F	20° C	
Boil Water	212° F	100° C	
Bake	325° F	160° C	3
	350° F	180° C	4
	375° F	190° C	5
	400° F	200° C	6
	425° F	220° C	7
	450° F	230° C	8
Broil			Grill

INDEX

A

Appetizers
Bruschetta, Tomato, 229
Dip, Muffuletta, 38
Guacamole with Grilled Corn,
Charred, 36
Nachos, Cowboy, 45
Shooters, Brisket, 49
Apples
Pork Loin, Apple-Kale Stuffed, 124
Sauce, Apple BBQ, 105
**Apricot-Chipotle Mayonnaise,
Dried, 154**
Artichokes, Grilled, 243
Asparagus, Kicked-Up Grilled, 238

B

Bacon
Hush Puppies, Bacon-and-
Caramelized Onion, 271
Mac and Cheese, Chipotle-
Bacon, 268
Relish, Cantaloupe-Bacon, 35
Satay, Chicken-and-Bacon, 174
Banana Pudding, 281
Beans
Baked Beans, Davenport Ranch
Cowboy, 263
Baked Beans, 3-Bean BBQ, 260
Nachos, Cowboy, 45
Salad, Black Bean and Grilled
Corn, 253
Beef. *See also* **Beef, Ground.**
  Brisket
    Brunswick Stew, Chicken-and-
    Brisket, 46
    Nachos, Cowboy, 45
    Sauce, Brisket Red, 42
    Shooters, Brisket, 49
    Smoked Brisket, Texas, 42
  Marinade, Beef, 24
  Ribs with Sorghum Glaze, Beef, 52

Steaks
Filet Mignon with Red Wine
Mushroom Sauce, Grilled, 89
Flank Steak, Lime-Cilantro, 113
Flank Steak Sandwiches with
Apple BBQ Sauce, 105
Flank Steak Skewers,
Lemon, 109
Flank Steak with Fig Salsa,
Rosemary, 115
Flank Steak with Watermelon
Salsa, Grilled Molasses, 110
Flat-Iron Steak, Balsamic-
Marinated, 106
Kabobs, Smoky Steak BBQ, 169
Kabobs with Jade Sauce, Curried
Beef, 101
Rib-eyes, Beer-and-Brown
Sugar, 98
Salad, Steak-and-Blue Cheese
Potato, 116
Skirt Steak, Mexican Grilled, 102
Strip Steaks, Blue Cheese-
Encrusted, 94
Tacos, Vietnamese BBQ, 97
Tri-Tip, Red Wine, 93
Tri-Tip with Citrus-Chile Butter,
Grilled, 90
Tenderloin, Marinated Beef, 86
Beef, Ground
Burgers, Pineapple-Jalapeño, 119
Hamburgers, Gorgonzola-
Stuffed, 120
Beverage
Lemonade, Grilled Rosemary, 226
Biscuit Pudding, 279
Bok Choy, Grilled, 240
Brined
Buttermilk-Brined Grilled
Chicken, 75
Dry-Brined Beer-Can Chicken, 68
Sweet-Tea Brined Chicken, 71
Bruschetta, Tomato, 229

Butter
Citrus Butter, 219
Citrus-Chile Butter, 90

C

Cabbage
Chowchow, 60
Casseroles
Mac and Cheese, Chipotle-Bacon,
268
Macaroni and Cheese, Classic
Baked, 264
Cheese
Green Tomatoes Caprese,
Grilled, 246
Grits, Grilled Peppers and Sausage
with Cheese, 153
Hamburgers, Gorgonzola-
Stuffed, 120
Mac and Cheese, Chipotle-
Bacon, 268
Macaroni and Cheese, Classic
Baked, 264
Nachos, Cowboy, 45
Salad, Steak-and-Blue Cheese
Potato, 116
Sandwiches
Pork Sandwiches, Italian
Grilled, 128
Smoked Turkey-Blue Cheese
Open-Faced Sandwiches, 80
Sauce, Blue Cheese, 183
Strip Steaks, Blue Cheese-
Encrusted, 94
Chicken
Breasts, Smothered Grilled
Chicken, 165
Breasts, Sweet Mustard-Glazed
Chicken, 162
  Brined
    Buttermilk-Brined Grilled
    Chicken, 75

Dry-Brined Beer-Can
Chicken, 68
Sweet-Tea Brined Chicken, 71
Brunswick Stew, Chicken-and-
Brisket, 46
Drumsticks, Lemon-Garlic, 182
Drumsticks, Spicy Honey-Lime
Grilled, 181
Grilled Sweet Guava Chicken, 76
Kabobs
Bacon Satay, Chicken-and-, 174
Curried Chicken Kabobs, 166
Jerk Chicken Kabobs, 170
Smoky Chicken BBQ Kabobs, 169
Quarters, Marinated Chicken, 158
South-of-the-Border BBQ
Chicken, 161
Thighs, Sweet Ginger Chicken, 178
Thighs, Sweet-Heat Boneless
Chicken, 177
Under a Skillet, Chicken, 72
Whole Chicken, Hickory-
Smoked, 67
Wings, Spicy Grilled, 182
Chowchow, 60
Collard Greens, 248
Corn
Chipotle Grilled Corn, 251
Grilled Corn, Charred Guacamole
with, 36
Hush Puppies, Shrimp-and-
Corn, 271
Salad, Black Bean and Grilled
Corn, 253
Cornish Hens, Asian-Grilled, 187
Cucumbers
Salsa, Grilled Grouper with
Cucumber-Watermelon, 199
Sauce, Cool Cucumber, 172

D

Desserts
Bars, Pecan Pie, 276
Cobbler, Summer Fruit, 275
Peaches with Whipped Cream and
Raspberry-Mint Mash,
Grilled, 272

Pudding, Banana, 281
Pudding, Biscuit, 279
Dry Rubs
All-Purpose BBQ Rub, 29
Brisket Dry Rub, 29
Cowgirl Pork Rub, 62
Ginger Rub, 51
Memphis Dry Rub, 28
Pork Dry Rub, 28
Smoky-Sweet BBQ Rub, 29

F

**Fig Salsa, Rosemary Flank Steak
with, 115**
Fish. See also **Salmon, Seafood,
Tuna.**
Catfish Fillets, Blackened
Grilled, 200
Grouper with Cucumber-
Watermelon Salsa,
Grilled, 199
Halibut, Garlic-and-Herb
Grilled, 194
Kabobs, Fish, 213
Sea Bass with Mango Salsa,
Grilled, 192
Swordfish with Olive-Basil Relish,
Grilled, 210
Tacos, Poblano Fish, 197
Fruit. See also **specific types.**
Cobbler, Summer Fruit, 275

G

Game
Quail, Asian-Grilled, 187
Garlic
Artichokes, Grilled, 243
Chicken, Grilled Sweet Guava, 76
Chicken Kabobs, Jerk, 170
Chicken, South-of-the-Border
BBQ, 161
Drumsticks, Lemon-Garlic, 182
Flank Steak, Lime-Cilantro, 113
Halibut, Garlic-and-Herb
Grilled, 194
Ratatouille, Grilled Vegetable, 233

Relish, Vidalia Onion and Peach
Refrigerator, 35
Sandwiches, Italian Grilled
Pork, 128
Shrimp Kabobs, Caribbean, 214
Tri-Tip, Red Wine, 93
Turkey, Papaw's Smoked, 79
Glazes
Citrus Teriyaki Glaze, 208
Guava Glaze, 76
Sorghum Glaze, Beef Ribs with, 52
Greens, Collard, 248
Grits
Brisket Shooters, 49
Cheese Grits, Grilled Peppers and
Sausage with, 153
**Guacamole with Grilled Corn,
Charred, 36**
Guava
Chicken, Grilled Sweet Guava, 76
Glaze, Guava, 76

H

Ham
Black-eyed Peas, 248
Collard Greens, 248
Honey
Drumsticks, Spicy Honey-Lime
Grilled, 181
Sauce, Spicy Honey-Lime BBQ, 181
Shrimp Kabobs, Honey-Lime
Grilled, 216
Hot Dogs, Sweet-Heat, 151
How to
Chop a Mango, 32
Peel & Devein Shrimp, 216
Peel & Grate Carrots, 245
Peel & Grate Ginger, 178
Peel, Seed & Chop Cucumber, 172
Peel, Slice & Mince Shallots, 254
Prepare a Charcoal Grill, 15
Seed & Mince Jalapeño
Peppers, 199
Seed a Tomato, 210
Shred Cabbage, 151
Whip Egg Whites to Stiff
Peaks, 281

Hush Puppies, 271
Jalapeño-Pineapple Hush
Puppies, 271
Shrimp-and-Corn Hush
Puppies, 271

K

Kabobs
Beef Kabobs with Jade Sauce,
Curried, 101
Chicken-and-Bacon Satay, 174
Chicken BBQ Kabobs,
Smoky, 169
Chicken Kabobs, Curried, 166
Chicken Kabobs, Jerk, 170
Fish Kabobs, 213
Flank Steak Skewers, Lemon, 109
Scallop Kabobs, Grilled, 221
Shrimp Kabobs, Caribbean, 214
Shrimp Kabobs, Honey-Lime
Grilled, 216
Steak BBQ Kabobs, Smoky, 169
Vegetable Kabobs, Grilled, 230
**Kale Stuffed Pork Loin,
Apple-, 124**
Ketchup, Mango, 27

L

Lemon
Drumsticks, Lemon-Garlic, 182
Flank Steak Skewers,
Lemon, 109
Lemonade, Grilled Rosemary, 226
Marinade, Lemon-Basil, 27
Sauce, Lemon Dipping, 109
Scallops, Lemony Herb-
Grilled, 219
Lime
Butter, Citrus, 219
Drumsticks, Spicy Honey-Lime
Grilled, 181
Flank Steak, Lime-Cilantro, 113
Sauce, Spicy Honey-Lime
BBQ, 181
Shrimp Kabobs, Honey-Lime
Grilled, 216

M

Macaroni
Baked Macaroni and Cheese,
Classic, 264
Chipotle-Bacon Mac and
Cheese, 268
Mangoes
Ketchup, Mango, 27
Salsa, Chipotle-Mango, 32
Salsa, Grilled Sea Bass with
Mango, 192
**Maple-and-Mustard Pork
Loin, 127**
Marinades
Asian Seafood Marinade, 24
Beef Marinade, 24
Lemon-Basil Marinade, 27
Sweet-and-Spicy Marinade, 24
**Mayonnaise, Dried Apricot-
Chipotle, 154**
Melons
Cantaloupe-Bacon Relish, 35
Watermelon
Salsa, Grilled Grouper with
Cucumber-Watermelon, 199
Salsa, Watermelon, 110
Sweet, Salty, and Spicy
Watermelon Refresher, 269
Microwave
Macaroni and Cheese, Classic
Baked, 264
Muffuletta Burgers, 188
Muffuletta Dip, 38
Mushrooms
Hamburgers, Gorgonzola-
Stuffed, 120
Sauce, Grilled Filet Mignon with
Red Wine Mushroom, 89
Stuffed Mushrooms, Grilled
Roasted Pepper-, 234
Mustard
Chicken Breasts, Sweet Mustard-
Glazed, 162
Pork Loin, Maple-and-
Mustard, 127
Sauce, Carolina Mustard BBQ, 22
Vinaigrette, Whole Grain
Mustard, 257

N

Nachos, Cowboy, 45

O

Olives
Burgers, Muffuletta, 188
Dip, Muffuletta, 38
Relish, Olive-Basil, 211
Onions
Caramelized Onion Hush Puppies,
Bacon-and-, 271
Vidalia Onion and Peach
Refrigerator Relish, 35
Vidalia Onion BBQ Sauce, 139
**Oysters with Spicy Cocktail Sauce,
Grilled, 222**

P

Pasta. *See also* **Macaroni.**
Salad, Tangy Tzatziki Pasta, 269
Peaches
Grilled Peaches with Whipped
Cream and Raspberry-Mint
Mash, 272
Pork Chops, Peach-Glazed, 142
Pulled Pork, Peach, 62
Relish, Vidalia Onion and Peach
Refrigerator, 35
Sauce, Brown Sugar Pork Chops
with Peach BBQ, 145
Peanut Sauce, 174
Peas, Black-eyed, 248
Pecans
Bars, Pecan Pie, 276
Pork Burgers with Dried Apricot-
Chipotle Mayonnaise, Pecan-
Crusted, 154
Peppers
Chile
Chipotle-Bacon Mac and
Cheese, 268
Chipotle-Cilantro Slaw, 245
Chipotle Grilled Corn, 251
Chipotle-Mango Salsa, 32
Chipotle Mayonnaise, Dried
Apricot-, 154

Chipotle Mayonnaise, Dried Apricot-, 154

Wings, Spicy Grilled, 182

Grilled Peppers and Sausage with Cheese Grits, 153

Jalapeño

Burgers, Pineapple-Jalapeño, 119

Cream, Cilantro-Jalapeño, 119

Hush Puppies, Jalapeño-Pineapple, 271

Sauce, Jade, 101

Poblano Fish Tacos, 197

Roasted Pepper-Stuffed Mushrooms, Grilled, 234

Pickles

Bread-and-Butter Pickles, Uncle Hoyt's, 148

Spicy Pickles, Pork Tenderloin Sliders with, 136

Sweet No-Cook Pickles, 149

Pico de Gallo, 45

Pineapple

Burgers, Pineapple-Jalapeño, 119

Hush Puppies, Jalapeño-Pineapple, 271

Tuna Steaks, Tropical Grilled, 203

Pitmasters

Helen Turner, Helen's BBQ, Brownsville, TN, 14

Nicole Davenport, Sheffield, TX, 63

Sam Jones, Skylight Inn, Ayden, NC, 279

Will Fleischman, Lockhart Smokehouse, Dallas, TX, 17

Pit Stops

Full Moon Bar-B-Que, Birmingham, AL, 116

Grady's Barbecue, Dudley, NC, 240

Oklahoma Joe's, Barbecue, Kansas City, KS, 207

Puckett's Grocery, Franklin, TN, 165

The Salt Lick, Driftwood, TX 79

Plum-Glazed Sausage, 146

Pork. *See also* **Bacon, Ham, Sausage.**

Burgers with Dried Apricot-Chipotle Mayonnaise, Pecan-Crusted Pork, 154

Chops

Brown Sugar Pork Chops with Peach BBQ Sauce, 145

Peach-Glazed Pork Chops, 142

Dry Rub, Pork, 28

Maple-and-Mustard Pork Loin, 127

Ribs

Baby Back Ribs, Glazed, 55

Baby Back Ribs, Sweet-and-Sour, 51

Country-Style Ribs, East Carolina, 140

Glazed Ribs, Championship, 56

Roasts

Pulled Pork, Peach, 62

Smoked Paprika Pork Roast with Sticky Stout BBQ Sauce, 64

Smoked Pork Butt, 59

Sandwiches, Italian Grilled Pork, 128

Sandwich, The Southern Living® Pulled Pork, 59

Steaks, Molasses-Glazed Pork, 146

Stuffed Pork Loin, Apple-Kale, 124

Tenderloin

Bourbon-Brown Sugar Pork Tenderloin, 134

Sandwiches, Grilled Pork Tenderloin, 139

Sliders with Spicy Pickles, Pork Tenderloin, 136

Sweet-and-Sour Pork Tenderloin, 133

Whiskey-Marinated Pork Tenderloin, 131

Potatoes. *See also* **Sweet Potatoes.**

Salads

Fingerling Potato Salad, Grilled, 256

Fresh Herb Potato Salad, 259

Steak-and-Blue Cheese Potato Salad, 116

Pudding, Banana, 281

Pudding, Biscuit, 279

Q

Quail, Asian-Grilled, 187

R

Raspberry-Mint Mash, Grilled Peaches with Whipped Cream and, 272

Ratatouille, Grilled Vegetable, 233

Relishes

Cantaloupe-Bacon Relish, 35

Chowchow, 60

Olive-Basil Relish, 211

Pico de Gallo, 45

Vidalia Onion and Peach Refrigerator Relish, 35

S

Salads and Salad Dressing

Black Bean and Grilled Corn Salad, 253

Pasta Salad, Tangy Tzatziki, 269

Potato Salad, Fresh Herb, 259

Potato Salad, Grilled Fingerling, 256

Steak-and-Blue Cheese Potato Salad, 116

Slaws

Chipotle-Cilantro Slaw, 245

Coleslaw, 49

Vinaigrette, Whole Grain Mustard, 257

Salmon

Sweet Asian-Grilled Salmon, 207

Teriyaki-Glazed Grilled Salmon, 208

Salsas

Chipotle-Mango Salsa, 32

Cucumber-Watermelon Salsa, Grilled Grouper with, 199

Fig Salsa, Rosemary Flank Steak with, 115

Grilled Salsa, 31

Mango Salsa, Grilled Sea Bass with, 192

Parsley-Mint Salsa Verde, 185

Burgers with Dried Apricot-Chipotle Mayonnaise, Pecan-Crusted Pork, 154
Flank Steak Sandwiches with Apple Barbecue Sauce, 105
Grilled Pork Tenderloin Sandwiches, 139
Grilled Tuna Sandwiches, 204
Hamburgers, Gorgonzola-Stuffed, 120
Open-Faced Sandwiches, Smoked Turkey-Blue Cheese, 80
Pulled Pork Sandwich, The Southern Living®, 59
Sliders with Spicy Pickles, Pork Tenderloin, 136

Sauces. *See also* **Glazes, Relishes, Salsas, Toppings.**
Apple Barbecue Sauce, 105
Blue Cheese Sauce, 183
Brisket Red Sauce, 42
Carolina Mustard BBQ Sauce, 22
Cocktail Sauce, Spicy, 222
Cucumber Sauce, Cool, 172
Eastern Carolina Vinegar Sauce, 22
Honey-Lime BBQ Sauce, Spicy, 181
Horseradish Cream Sauce, 86
Jade Sauce, 101
Kansas City BBQ Sauce, 23
Lemon Dipping Sauce, 109
Peach BBQ Sauce, Brown Sugar Pork Chops with, 145
Peanut Sauce, 174
Red Wine Mushroom Sauce, Grilled Filet Mignon with, 89
Sriracha Rémoulade, 27
Sticky Stout BBQ Sauce, 65
Sweet-and-Sour 'Cue Sauce, 51
Tomato BBQ Sauce, Sweet-and-Tangy, 59
Vidalia Onion BBQ Sauce, 139
Vietnamese Dipping Sauce, 97
White BBQ Sauce, 23

Sausage
Andouille Sausage with Pickles, Grilled, 148

Grilled Peppers and Sausage with Cheese Grits, 153
Plum-Glazed Sausage, 146

Scallops
Kabobs, Grilled Scallop, 221
Lemony Herb-Grilled Scallops, 219

Seafood. *See also* **Fish, Oysters, Shrimp.**
Marinade, Asian Seafood, 24

Shallots, Pickled, 257

Shrimp
Hush Puppies, Shrimp-and-Corn, 271
Kabobs, Caribbean Shrimp, 214
Kabobs, Honey-Lime Grilled Shrimp, 216

Sides. *See also* **Hush Puppies, Pickles, Salads and Salad Dressing.**
Artichokes, Grilled, 242
Asparagus, Kicked-Up Grilled, 238
Baked Beans, Davenport Ranch Cowboy, 263
Baked Beans, 3-Bean BBQ, 260
Black-eyed Peas, 248
Cheese Grits, Grilled Peppers and Sausage with, 153
Collard Greens, 248
Corn, Charred Guacamole with Grilled, 36
Corn, Chipotle Grilled, 251
Green Tomatoes Caprese, Grilled, 246
Mac and Cheese, Chipotle-Bacon, 268
Macaroni and Cheese, Classic Baked, 264
Mushrooms, Grilled Roasted Pepper-Stuffed, 234
Ratatouille, Grilled Vegetable, 233
Shallots, Pickled, 257
Sweet Potatoes on the Grill, 253
Sweet Potato Fluff, 278
Sweet Potato Planks, Grilled, 254
Tomato Bruschetta, 229
Vegetable Kabobs, Grilled, 230
Watermelon Refresher, Sweet, Salty, and Spicy, 269

Zucchini, Sweet-Grilled, 237
Spreads
Butter, Citrus, 219
Butter, Citrus-Chile, 90
Mayonnaise, Dried Apricot-Chipotle, 154
Sriracha Rémoulade, 27
Stew, Chicken-and-Brisket Brunswick, 46
Sweet Potatoes
Fluff, Sweet Potato, 278
Grilled Sweet Potato Planks, 254
Grill, Sweet Potatoes on the, 253

T

Tacos
Fish Tacos, Poblano, 197
Vietnamese Barbecue Tacos, 97
Teriyaki Glaze, Citrus, 208
Teriyaki-Glazed Grilled Salmon, 208
Tips from Troy 38
allowing roast to stand, 127
ancho chile powder, 161
baking ribs, 52
boneless skinless chicken thighs, 177
brine, 145
brining poultry, 71
broiling tuna steaks, 204
buying pork tenderloins, 131
buying raw shrimp, guidelines for, 214
cheese sauce, 264
chicken pieces already cut up, 158
cooking pasta, 268
cooking potatoes for potato salad, 259
cooking sweet potatoes to mash, 278
country-style ribs, 140
cuts of chicken, 76
doubling a recipe, 263
dry rub ingredients, 64
farm-raised catfish fillets, 200
flank steak, 109
flat-iron steak, 106

cuts of chicken, 76

doubling a recipe, 263

dry rub ingredients, 64

farm-raised catfish fillets, 200

flank steak, 109

flat-iron steak, 106

following quick-grilling recipes, 15

grilling zucchini, 237

Italian olive salad, 38

leftover turkey, 80

marinate time, 113

pastry crust, 276

peeling garlic, 194

saving time, 257

seasoning filets, 89

shredding chicken, 46

smoker times, 11

soft breadcrumbs, 94

Sweet No-Cook Pickles, 149

tri-tip roast, 93

Tomatoes

Bruschetta, Tomato, 229

Green Tomatoes Caprese,
    Grilled, 246

Pico de Gallo, 45

Sauce, Sweet-and-Tangy Tomato
    BBQ, 59

Tools of the Trade

Charcoal

Briquettes, Charcoal, 14

Grills, Charcoal, 10

How to Prepare a Charcoal
    Grill, 15

Lump Charcoal, 14

Gas Grills, 10

Grilling Basics

Direct Heat Grilling, 17

Indirect Heat Grilling, 17

Smokers, 11

Troy's Top 10 Tools

Basting Brushes & Mops, 13

Chimney Starter, 13

Disposable Foil Pans, 13

Grill Brush, 13

Insulated Barbecue Mitts, 13

Kitchen Timer, 13

Spatulas, 13

Spray Bottle, 13

Thermometers, 13

Tongs, 13

Wood

Smoking Basics, 19

Wood Chips, 19

Wood Chunks, 19

Toppings

Cilantro-Jalapeño Cream, 119

Mango Ketchup, 27

Tuna

Sandwiches, Grilled Tuna, 204

Steaks, Tropical Grilled
    Tuna, 203

Turkey

Burgers, Muffuletta, 188

Breast, Citrus-Grilled Turkey, 83

Breast, Grilled Turkey, 184

Sandwiches, Smoked Turkey-Blue
    Cheese Open-Faced, 80

Smoked Turkey, Papaw's, 79

Tzatziki Pasta Salad, Tangy, 269

V

Vegetables. *See also* **specific types.**

Kabobs, Grilled Vegetable, 230

Ratatouille, Grilled Vegetable, 233

Salad, Tangy Tzatziki Pasta, 269

Salsa, Grilled, 31

Z

Zucchini, Sweet-Grilled, 237